For Alison,
with respect and gratitude.
You haven't seen the last
of me! Warmly,

THE LAST OF HER

A FORENSIC MEMOIR

Published by Jaded Ibis Press.
http://www.jadedibispress.com

 JADED IBIS PRESS

""And yet they, who passed away long ago, still exist in us, as predisposition, as burden upon our fate, as murmuring blood, and as gesture that rises up from the depths of time."
    —*Rainer Maria Rilke, Letters to a Young Poet,*
        trans. by Stephen Mitchell

"For five days I lie in secret"
    —*Sylvia Plath, "Face Lift"*

For Jason Kupperman and Keiko Rosenbaum

CONTENTS

PREFACE

"It's the last luxury. To go early and never come back."

"Have a good life," my mother wrote in March 1989, at the bottom of page four of her nineteen-page suicide letter.

This final communication, addressed to me, contained detailed instructions concerning renovations to her co-op apartment in Manhattan, who to rent the back bedroom to and why I should live there; what to tell the attorney handling her fraudulent insurance case (that I was her sister and she had no daughter); what to tell the lawyer who had drawn up the will (that I was absolutely her daughter); what to call the story about her life as a child with spina bifida (Born Dead); how to market the makeup line, Exclusively Yours, which she had conceptualized; who should receive her mink coat and designer dresses; and who to notify (and in what order).

Almost twenty pages of specifics about attorneys, real estate, projects, clothing, and telephone calls. Yet to me, her only daughter and immediate next of kin, she wrote five sentences summarizing the future, present, and past of our relationship:

> My spirit will always be with you. Sorry I couldn't go through all the surgery I would have to have. The pain now is too much. Sorry I wasn't a healthy mother—but that was the roll of the dice in life. I love you and I'm sorry you'll have so much to do.

Dolores killed herself on March 29, 1989 (just several months' shy of her sixtieth birthday), but her dying had been put in motion decades before. Long after she died, I started to identify days and events pivotal in her unraveling. For example, March 19, 1969: On this day, after twelve months of trying to convince a New York State Supreme Court judge that chronic physical pain did not make her an unfit mother (though it necessitated pain medication and frequent hospitalization), the justice concluded that she was, as a parent, maybe not flawed beyond repair, but damaged enough to be dangerous. And thus he severed us. I don't mean to pretend that we were emotionally joined; my mother was absent psychically and/or physically when I was in her custody. I didn't know much about her until after we were separated, and I wouldn't have much compassion for her until long after she died. I only vaguely understood that the judge's decision to remove me from her custody altered our circumstances—I saw her every other weekend and for half the summer and some holidays. She became bitter and manipulated me, first into believing I wanted to live with her and then into acting out desperate dramas—a disappearance, running away—that she concocted. For her, these scripted acts of false rebellion ended in a contempt citation from the court and supervised visitation. But for me, they resulted in appreciating that lying was ugly and unproductive. It followed that our relationship deteriorated as I grew older and began to recognize, and then resent and disdain, her inability not only to tell the truth but to be inside a day without premeditating every interaction with other people.

Few are the documented facts about my mother's life before my father and I appeared in it. She had her own fictionalized versions of what happened on each of the decisive days I've identified, days described in newspaper articles and court, law enforcement, and census records:

On April 8, 1958, she was arrested for assaulting a pregnant woman; at the time she worked for a distributor of diet pills, but she had been a cosmetics industry executive. Seven years before that—on March 19, 1951—her mother died from complications related to multiple sclerosis in a hospital for the indigent in Rochester, NY. My mother's birth certificate confirms a birthdate, June 4, 1929, in Newark, New Jersey. Federal and state census and city records show that she lived for at least several years in Rochester with her mother and maternal grandmother, who was deaf. Her father was incarcerated in Cincinnati in 1940, but then joined his wife and daughter in Rochester. He didn't stay long; he made his way, alone, to New York City, where he was arrested in September of 1947 for running a rigged dice game.

The last two decades of Dolores's life started in 1969, when, at close to forty years old, unemployed, single, and disabled, a court clerk filed the New York State Supreme Court judge's ruling that removed me from her home. She talked about appealing the decision immediately after it was made. In the early seventies, she even married again, thinking the union would prove to the court that her home was a stable environment (she was convinced that being single was one of the main reasons for the court's decision, and in retrospect, I have to agree it was likely a factor). Her new husband died of a heart attack on Halloween day while riding a commuter train. For a time, I wondered if she had killed him. If that seems like a stretch, remember that she was indicted for attacking a pregnant woman; I was fairly convinced she purposely caused a fire in her apartment in the early 1980s to collect an insurance pay-out. And I discovered, after she died, how many aliases she maintained and the extent of her fraudulent activities.

After divorcing my father, my mother changed her name back to Dolores E. Buxton (her actual maiden name had been Buxbaum, which her father had changed, though I don't know exactly when). Buxton was the name she used as the savvy cosmetics executive she had been in the 1950s; in the 1970s, she recast Miss Buxton as a film-production and editorial consultant. Dolores B. Wender was the widow who received disability and became a central character in the 1980s. And then she fashioned KD Buxton, an amalgam of my mother and myself, who appeared after I had moved to France in the mid-1980s to go to school, and was the pen name she planned to use on the books she outlined but never finished writing.

As my mother saw things, her end was merely "a bad roll of the dice," an interesting phrase given her father's lifelong vocation as card shark, pool hustler, and confidence man. A supposition is inherent in such a phrase, that fate trumps free will, that she was powerless to shape her life. Many years had to pass after my mother's suicide before I was able to think of her not solely as the person closest to me who had wronged me most profoundly by killing herself. I agreed with Arthur Miller, that "Suicide kills two people," and I thought for a long time that Dolores had killed part of me.

To undo that kind of psychic filicide meant examining—with a forensic attention—who my mother had been and why she made the choices she made. Which led me to consider what had happened to Dolores before she told her first lie and worked her first scam. How is the interior life furnished when it belongs to someone who has learned truth does not always result in getting what you want? I didn't know much about Dolores as a young woman, though I suspected she had become practiced at the art of lying by the time she was in her late teens. And I knew nothing of her girlhood save her romanticized and scant tales, though photos attested to the fact that she and her mother, Dorothy, lived for a time with her deaf grandmother in Rochester, New York, which is where my maternal great-grandparents lived, met, married, had children, and where one had died and was buried.

In mid-August of 2012, I drove north, to see what I could see of what remains of my mother's family in Rochester: the gravesites of her mother and grandfather. Route 15 hugs the western side of the Susquehanna River, and I looked to the red-tailed hawks flying along the riverbank as a promise of clarity to come. Once arrived in Monroe County, New York, I made my way toward the city where my mother, grandmother, and great-grandmother had lived together at the same time, a place that I, as daughter, granddaughter, and great-granddaughter invested with the mythos of ancestry, though it is only later that I would identify it as a place that both my relations fled. My grandmother to New Jersey, where she met and married my grandfather. My mother to New York City then California, in pursuit of the same man, her father. The day I arrived, thunderstorms were predicted. I stopped and walked along the Genesee River, and the first bird I saw was a blue heron.

Herons always seem to materialize from an imperceptible layer behind the scenes. Nothing is ambiguous about their raspy croaks, which command you to stop what you're doing and look up. The one at the river passed silently at first; it seemed to have been projected out from the solid expanse of immobile cloud. Another flap of the enormous wings and it released one long syllable, chiseling the silence. In the empty space left behind, the wind riffled the trees and the rain tap-tap-spattered, and the entire orchestration belonged to that bird, the messenger aloft. The sky roiled and darkened with the accelerating storm.

Once you come face to face with a heron, you watch for them. Or, at least that's what happened to me after coming so close to one I might have touched it by extending my arm. It stood in the middle of a road I had turned down in error. It stood so still that the backward S-curve of its neck seemed articulated of petrified wood rather than living flesh. Its solitary amber eye dilated, and as the bird registered the level of my threat, I gawked, startled by how artificial, how carved it seemed, as if the landscape behind it were fashioned of stone. When the heron unfolded its enormous slate-blue wings and lifted off the ground, I expected a hushed sigh of feathers, but instead there was a silence as old as shale. The kind of non-sound that implies an instant release from the terrestrial. That night I dreamt about the dead.

Once I arrived in Rochester, I drove directly to Mt. Hope, the country's first municipal Victorian cemetery, where my mother's maternal grandfather, Albert, is buried. I had planned to walk around, but after a brief amble, decided to motor instead, what with the threatening weather and the immensity of the place, the roads meandering, and the terrain more hilly than not. Lightning flashed on the horizon, and I returned to my car. I drove up and down several of the cemetery's steep and narrow inclines. Raindrops splashed and just as rapidly stopped, only to start again, and I drove around some more, but the signage was either turned the wrong way or barely legible, and Mt. Hope's office was closed. I made my way to the exit, passing fallen tree limbs, toppled-over gravestones, and a large scummy pond. In spite of the disorder and disrepair, under the canopy of these tall hardwoods and sloping evergreens and above them the sky like boiled cotton, the place enchanted me.

I decided to cross the city and visit Holy Sepulchre Cemetery, where my mother's mother, Dorothy, the grandmother I never knew, is buried. Past Kodak's world headquarters and High Falls, on a road that leads to Lake Ontario, is the strictly ordered, flatter Catholic burial ground. Not a blade of grass seemed out of place. On an index card, I'd printed the information needed to locate Dorothy Buxbaum: section North 26, tier four, grave number twelve. I wondered if my grandfather and then mother had changed their surname to Buxton before or after my grandmother died. And if she was still alive when they did, why she, a Catholic woman, had kept this Jewish name after her divorce from my grandfather.

Each marble and granite marker had been austerely placed and stood upright, clean and readable. Some were decorated with still-new flowers. The act of visiting a place where family once resided and are now buried is infused with the most solemn satisfaction. Which faded when I realized I had brought nothing to leave in remembrance of the grandmother I never knew. And disappeared when I understood there was no marked grave.

At section North 26, tier four, all the markers are small granite rectangles laid flat in the grass. Like Dorothy, everyone in this row died in 1951. Number twelve was at the periphery of the base of a sapling, yet there was no marker. *Walk back to the start of the row and count again,* I told myself. And again, an ache of disbelief nestled into my sacrum, spreading out like a hand pressed against the small of my back.

As I acknowledged this unmarked spot as where my grandmother was interred, four deer sprinted across another section of the cemetery. A fifth lingered and browsed. On catching my human scent, she lifted her head, and looked toward the sapling where I stood, distracted. An instant later, the doe bounded off in the direction of her herd. A crow sounded from within the thickly leafed treetops, as if the white tail flashing in the dusk had been an intruder to its high nest. When I gazed again at the ground, the sequence—arrival, birds, storm, deer, bird—seemed like some kind of message but made no sense to me.

Underneath my feet were the scant remains of Dorothy, cast in the role of Unknown-Beautiful-Kind Grandmother Who Died Very Young of MS. She had been lowered into an unmarked grave I am sure my mother never visited, at the base of a tree that wasn't there at the time of burial. *What did you expect to find?* I asked myself. No discovery would be mine until the next day, when I returned to Mt. Hope and located my great-grandfather Albert's grave, which, like Dorothy's (his only daughter), is also unmarked and unremarkably situated in what must be the flattest part of an otherwise undulating cemetery. As I stood at his burial site, I felt a brief gliding across time, the sensing-without-knowing that the reptilian brain offers, which must have tremored at the nape of Dorothy's neck or tightened in the small of her back when she came to this place to remember her father and saw that intolerably bare rectangle of grass. The true revelation came after, long after, when I finally felt the weight of apprehending a key fact about women on the maternal side of my family. Namely that, across generations, they all endured hardship, physical and psychological traumas; they all died alone, mostly of heartbreak, none of them able to sustain happiness with another person for more than several years.

When I arrived at my great-grandfather Albert's gravesite, three crows alit on the macadam. They proceeded to waddle, each in its own direction, as if they were the true custodians of these grounds, pranksters who wait in places such as these to play benign tricks on the unwary. And why not these jester corvids precisely at this moment? For me they are totems that signal import (I've never encountered a crow who didn't presage or emphasize an experience), though I must admit that the absurdist part of my mind was visualizing the Three Stooges meet Heckle and Jeckle. Such humorous images comfort me and as I stood there, I thought about all the pictures of my great-grandparents. In each one, laughter plays across their faces, despite adversities I can only, literally, imagine. Both child immigrants, one deaf while crossing the Atlantic, the other losing his hearing after arrival in America, both given up, as deaf children were in those days, to a residential school. And yet they married, had a home here, a life, and made a child. A brief happiness was theirs.

At the unmarked grave of a man who is part of the equation that equals my grandmother Dorothy and thus my mother, Dolores, and which ends with me, I thought of a particular photograph in which my great-grandfather is smiling at his only daughter. It is a picture of summer: young men and their wives, all of them wearing hats, sitting on the steps of a cottage at Lake Ontario's Sodus Point. It appears as if my grandmother—not more than two years old in this image—is signing a word, perhaps her first. Father and daughter are caught inside one another's gaze to the exclusion of everyone else in the picture. No one is alive to know exactly what catalyzed that instant of father and daughter so entranced, but it was a destination arrived at after a series of many long silences both figurative and real: As a small child, my great-grandfather Albert had traveled from the interior of the European continent to its edge and sailed across an ocean. The train brought him northwest through New York State and its farmlands into the riverine city of Rochester, with its waterfalls and flour mills. He was trapped in deafness and emancipated by sign language; taken into a school, where he learned type setting and carpentry, and let out of it into marriage and fatherhood. After all these small victories, at age twenty-nine, he climbed onto a rooftop, a hammer in the leather tool belt around his waist, slipped, and fell. The impact cracked open his skull.

After the useless detour at the hospital, he was brought here, to what was then an eight-dollar cemetery plot, "laid to rest," as the phrase goes, though one must wonder if the dead ever repose when we keep bringing them back to life and reimagining their demise.

"Here the birds' journey ends," writes the poet Mahmoud Darwish. A line that I came to understand in a Rochester cemetery on an August day 101 years after my great-grandfather Albert's death. Like other excursions I have made involving my relations, this one involved creatures with wings. Birds are always somewhere when I've embarked thusly in my mind, circling, perched, hopping, calling, soaring. How can one not take stock of certain things that resurface when attempting to untangle the otherwise unknowable reasons for a life becoming one thing or another, often not what was planned or desired? In a way, that's what this entire exercise in exhuming Dolores's past has been, a scrutiny of the endless mystery of her private life, a story I will never *really* know.

The trek to Rochester started with hawks, the keen-sighted circling from on high. In between: the lone heron messenger carving itself out of the clouds. One alarmed crow in the wooded canopy. In finale, a gang of crows: three tricksters of the graveyard with a fluster of shiny feathers, strutting across the path. Is it any surprise that I might look to the sky and find not God, but wings spread against that atmospheric vault and all its furnishings—tree lines, mountain peaks, vanishing points, the rising and setting of celestial bodies? Perhaps it is enough to attend to such moments, full as they are of the little inscrutabilities one cannot solve.

My preoccupation with flight and all its manifestations—ascension and departure; to rise above and lose one's grounding; to flee—must end, lest it trap me and my daughter self in the endless O of sorrow. To let go of something that is carried for a long time requires practice.

DAY 1:
This is My Play's Last Scene

This is the song of our last meeting.
I looked back at the shape of the dark house.
Candles guttered in the bedroom window,
indifferent, yellow.

> — *Anna Akhmatova, "Song of the Last Meeting,"*
> *trans. by Stephen Berg [March 29, 1989]*

I. "like investigating mercury vapour in order to comprehend the nature of vapours."

Two months before my mother killed herself in March of 1989, I severed all contact with her. Dolores was almost sixty, and her orchestration of several scams, including Medicare fraud and a bogus insurance claim, had reached critical mass. In the last months of 1988, a claims adjustor—improbably named Mr. Tell—had stumbled upon several inconsistencies in my mother's story about a robbery, which she described as happening in broad daylight while taking her jewelry to the bank's safe deposit box. In one version, Dolores said the perpetrator was dressed in a black sweatshirt; in another account, he was wearing a red T-shirt. At first, he was on foot and used a gun; later he was riding a bicycle when he snatched her bag. Mr. Tell, without the aid of today's ubiquitous search-engine technology, did what he was trained to do: made phone calls, followed paper trails, walked the route of the supposed crime scene, and in the course of doing his job accidentally discovered that Dolores Buxton was using a number of different aliases and had filed several claims with the same company. What had started as a seemingly routine report of jewelry theft evolved into a tangle of lies, complete with depositions under oath conducted in Dolores's apartment on West Seventieth Street in Manhattan.

My mother's life came to this tipping point after years of disability, physical and emotional pain, and subsequent narcotics use and dependency, all of which she pointed to when justifying the dishonesty of her subsistence. She navigated the margins in so many ways that she had become not quite predatory, but opportunistic, much like the coyote who lives on the edges created by an encroaching urban landscape. By the last years of the 1980s, like the city itself, Dolores was drained, transformed into a wasteland she prowled as a bitter outlaw who had blundered and knew it, with the kind of desperate regret from which no good shall come.

She died in late March of 1989, but the current crisis that led her to suicide began in November 1988, not long after my twenty-ninth birthday. I was at the time living on West 109th Street and working in a specialized library at Barnard College. Like many my age before and since, I pretended to know more than I really knew and did as I pleased. I cavorted with the dalliance du jour into the "rat hours," as I called that time between night and day in the city, all in an attempt to build a world whose only cadence was pleasure but in which emotional ties were severed more often than not. These careless physical interludes were unfulfilled and unfulfilling, and made of my body a landscape that perfectly reflected the shameless solipsism that defined not only the spirit of the decade, but the island metropolis on which I lived and where I had been born and spent my childhood.

Even toward the end, when Dolores had stopped making appearances in public, she was still quite stunning, if you knew how to see who she had been underneath the artifice she practiced. By the time Mr. Tell arrived at her door to investigate the insurance claim, which he did some time during the winter of 1988-89, her dyed-blonde hair was coiffed, gently pulled back from the forehead into loose curls that fell to her shoulders, accentuating her high cheekbones and the uninterrupted oval of her face. Her skin was made matte with liquid foundation and powdered into an inscrutable paleness, the cheeks barely rouged, as if the involuntary effort of breathing had caused her to blush. The contrast of her dark brown eyes against this ivoried palette—the eyelids lined in black, lashes heavily mascaraed, brows penciled—was a sort of tenebrism, that pronounced chiaroscuro employed to great dramatic effect by painters such as El Greco, Caravaggio, and Gentileschi, in which the darkest and lightest elements are purposefully and violently contrasted. But because Dolores did not want your eye drawn to hers for too long, a splash of bright red across her lined and lipsticked mouth pulled your gaze downward and away, the color made more vivid by a black sweater and slacks, chosen to give the impression that she was comfortable but serious.

But before Mr. Tell ever knocked on her door, she had telephoned me. "You need to come and testify for me, Kim," Dolores said. Her voice, deepened from a lifetime of smoking, betrayed no panic, but something urgent in her pitch put me on alert.

"I've told the insurance agent that you're my sister, and that *our* mother, Dorothy Albrecht, has dementia and currently resides in a Florida nursing home."

Though my mother's ability to lie had ceased to surprise, this particular disordering of the truth stunned me. I never knew my maternal grandmother, but according to my mother, Dorothy Buxbaum had died of multiple sclerosis at age thirty-six, when Dolores, who claimed to have interrupted her own life to care for her dying mother, was nineteen. Albrecht was the last name of the man who was the caretaker of a brownstone at St. Luke's Place, where my mother had lived for a brief time in the 1960s. Jack Albrecht had been convicted of child molestation. He was not a man I liked, and, I suspected, my grandmother Dorothy, whom my mother unfailingly characterized as a selfless, beautiful, and humble woman, wouldn't have approved of him either.

"I need your help," Dolores said, and as she spoke, I detected a quality in her voice that she employed when I was younger, a tone limned of magnetism and threat, the kind of forceful energy that is difficult to resist and harder to disengage.

"I'll have to think about it," I said. But I already *knew* my thoughts on the matter: none of what she was telling me was good, and I didn't intend to play. My mother did not have a sister. My grandmother had kept my grandfather's surname; he was the one man she had married and then divorced (a man, it turned out, who shared Jack Albrecht's taste for young girls); she did not, nor had she ever, lived in Florida. Jack Albrecht was dead and so was my grandfather. If Dolores's plan of reviving the dead to assist the living hadn't involved me, and if I hadn't known the truth, the story she was spinning might have seemed darkly comic.

But it wasn't funny, and I knew this even in the fog of my twenty-somethingness. Looking back, I think the story frightened me because of its lack of nuance.

As a young adult, I chose the path of least resistance when dealing with my mother, and, to a lesser degree, with my father and stepmother, Phoebe. Which meant that I avoided all three of them as much as I could, hiding behind the autonomy-driven bravado bequeathed us in these modern times. Before the insurance investigation, my mother and I had cultivated a cordial relationship, which was unsatisfying to us both for different reasons. My inability to acknowledge what she christened her "pain" must have seemed like a failure on my part to empathize with her dissatisfaction and unhappiness. Her inability to see that her masquerade embarrassed me eluded my comprehension. I lived in a neighborhood that was rough enough to keep her away. She lived in a six-room apartment on a block where muggings, robberies, drugs, and prostitution had once been commonplace, and whose gentrification was beginning to define it as upscale. Dolores embraced this environmental change as she had embraced playing the role of the disabled single mother who had, in 1968, moved into what was, back then, welfare housing on West Seventieth Street. I saw her during brief visits and holidays. She sent me money. We didn't watch movies or go out together. She avoided the sun and disliked walking. I didn't think there was anything she could teach me. Or, perhaps more accurately, there was nothing I wanted to learn from her, least of all how to construct labyrinthine stories from which no exit was possible.

The insurance investigation had spooked her, and she was on the verge of having to depend on me, which caused her to despair and, in turn, shook the edges of my world, which was small, but seemed all important in that way one's surroundings seem when you're twenty-something. When my mother started calling me hourly at work, I tensed. We argued. I hung up on her. She called back. We repeated this routine throughout the day.

"I can't talk to you now," I said.

Dolores's calls were so frequent and disruptive that my boss summoned me to her office for an official reprimand.

I looked at the floor as she talked and imagined myself in a *Star Trek* episode. At any minute, I'd be beamed up to the spaceship hovering above the Earth.

"No more personal calls," she said.

"You don't understand," I answered. "These are not calls I've invited. My mother, she's unstable, she's mentally—"

"No more personal calls." This woman, who had authored a savvy analysis of the Triangle Shirtwaist Fire, was possessed of an unruly mass of wiry hair, which she had recently dyed a dark shade of purple—*aubergine*, it was called, and which stood out as incongruent with her rigidity. What kind of woman, I wondered, can be such a bitch with hair the color of an eggplant?

I nodded.

When she couldn't reach me at my office, my mother, unrelenting, called me at home. I despised her intrusion into my hours, the disruption it caused, and the anxiety I started to feel every time the phone rang.

"Mom, I can't lie for you," I said one day. My statement triggered a full minute of silence before she uttered a terse good-bye and hung up.

She could have said she was sorry, but she didn't and besides, what would an apology really have accomplished?

My refusal to play a part she had written for me infuriated her, and as her anger strengthened, the number of daily calls increased. When she started to telephone me at work again, I took to hanging up before she finished saying my name.

The last conversation with my mother concerned an insurance investigation, yet nothing about our final exchange protected anything of value, nor did it uncover what would remain hidden, which is to say the truth, itself larger and possibly more complex than the elaborate deception Dolores had coordinated.

II. "no refuge from confession but suicide; and suicide is confession."

Final conversations are often mundane—how can we ever anticipate the last sentence we say or hear? If you're lucky, both speaker and listener are lucid and honest and some mystery is elucidated or some gift of emotional expression exchanged. That last conversation with Dolores startled me. I'd never really know what motivated her to enact the fraud she was perpetrating. But later I'd pinpoint that click of the call ending as the beginning of how I started pondering how Dolores had become a woman whose world, image, and even memory were constructed of nothing but lies. At the time, however, that last phone conversation was simply one more scene in a series of dramatic and uncomfortable talks we had before she died.

What must have been on her mind then? After she placed the handset in the cradle, was she already thinking about suicide as the only way she could escape the trap she was in? Was she already wondering how exactly to pull it off? Thinking she'd have to make her death look as if it were from natural causes so as to inflict the most guilt on her daughter? A selfish daughter deserved to feel guilty. Digoxin, she knew, slowed the heart. She'd be sure to read more about it. There were the windows to be installed, which would increase the value of the apartment. The dog, of course, needed a new home. She trembled slightly considering all the instructions she'd have to write (to the selfish though beloved daughter,

31

she thought, with a romantic but misconstrued tenderness), about carrying through some of her ideas, some of which were potential goldmines, all of which would ensure a certain legacy. The cleaning of the house, that would have to happen, but not too obsessively if her death was going to seem "natural," which suddenly sounded ridiculous—what was natural about dying? No need to debate things. Be practical: there was some cash to distribute, not much, but enough to leave tips for the superintendent and porter who worked in the building. Can't forget to call Goodrich Pharmacy and tell them not to deliver the next refill on her medications. Such banalities to contemplate when planning one's death.

Then, did she recall her predicament, namely that her life was splitting open, exactly like Muriel Rukeyser promised if one woman told the truth about her life? Though, of course, she wasn't telling the truth. Mr. Tell was discovering it, and she was trying to alter what he found.

Or did she dismiss all of it as too much to do? Did she enlist that reliable psychic state we call denial and tune out the conflict with me, willfully summon an entirely different thought? Did she turn on the television to see if her lottery number had come in? Did she reach for the emery board and start filing the nail that had chipped just an hour ago? Was she contemplating a memory she *hadn't* invented?

My mother was a baby during the Depression. Just after she was born, her father was laid off from a legitimate job and was starting to learn a hustle or two. She was walking and talking when President Hoover told Americans the worst was over (of course it wasn't). She came of age during the Second World War, dating, dancing, sitting in classrooms, walking home from school in Rochester, New York. A career woman at the start of the fifties, she was pregnant by the end of the decade and, as a divorced single mother in the 1960s through the 1970s, she dated different men in varying degrees of seriousness, from one or two dinners or movies to living together and once even marriage. The men were diverse: an artist, a magazine editor, an impresario, a Wall Street broker, a musician, an insurance salesman. She had a lot of real memories to summon, complete with rich images and sounds rooted in history, and she was witness to profound changes in technology.

In her lifetime she watched the unfolding of three wars, which shaped the history of the modern world in ways we are just now beginning to fathom. She saw typewriters go from manual to electric to electronic; telephones morph from dial to push button, stationary to portable. She watched hemlines go up, practically vanish, and come down again. She knew how to wear both hats and gloves, show off a bare head and hands, be sleeved and sleeveless. Yet with of all this knowledge at her disposal, she centered her stories on untruths about her own life. If I had asked her what she had seen in the world beyond her, the possibilities are endless as to what she might have told me. But I never asked or had the presence of mind to listen if she had hinted in any way that she'd want to tell me such things. Instead, we were trapped in the singular and fabricated version of her private world, one in which she had been wronged and had no responsibility for her own undoing.

"Remember, Kim," she had said the day we spoke to one another for the last time, "when the investigator calls, you *have* to tell him that you are my sister—"

"I'm not doing this. Please don't ask me. Don't you see how screwed up it all sounds?"

She didn't see because she couldn't. Her focus was instead on forcing truth into the story to make it work. After she died, I sorted through her notes and read the deposition, learning that the role she enacted for Mr. Tell was that of a corporate executive.

"I've learned," she wrote in notes she had prepared for her testimony, "that Top Management doesn't know what goes on right under its nose. The government (U.S.A.) doesn't, and I have also seen how even lawyers and doctors, school officials, etc., are just as prone to stress and burn-out as an airline pilot."

Okay, sure, she *was* right about some things. But she was impetuous, and her ideas were disconnected. She had plenty to teach me, if I had been interested in learning how to lie in order to survive, or, perhaps, if I had been more patient with her, or if I had realized that nothing could ever melt the thing that glaciered around her heart and trapped her inside her own stories.

Each decade of Dolores's life offered the listener of her tales any number of accomplishments: model and DJ in her teens, real-estate mogul turned beauty-industry corporate executive in her twenties, film producer in her thirties, backgammon champion and publisher in her forties. By the time Dolores reached her fifties, the stories took on a cliché sepia tone as she declined, a turning inward made manifest by her frequent retreat into a darkened bedroom in the back of her apartment on West Seventieth Street. She spun so many tales: The "revolutionary" and "experimental" medical intervention—devised by a doctor cousin—which allowed her to overcome a congenital spinal defect and not be bound to a wheelchair. Her father's work in "real estate," which explained why she had (according to her) attended schools in thirty-three states. Her supposed intimacies with the famous (Frank Sinatra) and infamous (O. Roy Chalk). She told anyone whose audience she had secured that she had once mingled closely (nose to nose? cheek to cheek?) with Hollywood celebrities (including Marilyn Monroe and Groucho Marx) and cultivated relationships with politicians (John F. Kennedy among them) and had she wished, she might have married one of her many suitors, including a curiously unnamed businessman who operated what Dolores called "Swiss banking cartels." When I first heard that particular phrase, I pictured a highly manicured man, impeccably dressed, broad-shouldered but not too tall, with a receding hairline tastefully managed, an obsessive drive for keeping things clean, and safety-deposit boxes full of gold and cash. Someone whose trouser creases were sharp enough to make you think they were folded from paper. Maybe that's who my mother imagined, too.

For the most part, storytelling allowed Dolores to direct and control the narrative while giving her a chance to play both the central character *and* the supporting roles. And in a way, she had managed to express a truth about the spirit of her age, an age in which women had entered public life but were expected to wear disguises, to keep anyone from seeing what happens when the elasticity of youth wanes. But just at that moment in 1989, the House of Dolores was coming down, and she was caught in the rush to save it from demolition. She was cornered, and I, her only child and closest next of kin, refused to assist her.

III. *"growing in the darkness like a lament or the rain."*

That final phone call signaled that this entire affair would become untenable if left it to play out according to my mother's design. I confided in Bob, a family friend and lawyer who bluntly advised me to stop communicating with Dolores.

"She's older and not well; you're young and healthy," he said. "You'll be the one who goes to jail if you're deemed complicit in her crimes."

Complicit. The minute Bob uttered the word, I archived it, though years passed before I discovered that my mother was trying to make me her accomplice, as her father had once made her his co-conspirator. At the time, I refused the call to complicity; my sense of being a desperado waned rapidly whenever circumstances made me feel as if being Dolores's daughter automatically rendered me a criminal. I knew about the fraud she was committing but didn't want to be held accountable for it. And she wanted to undo an unsatisfying relationship with her only child without killing me, so she erased me in her narrative and rendered me a fictional sister.

Physically, thirty-nine city blocks separated my mother and me. This is a relatively short distance—almost two miles. Fifteen to twenty minutes, door to door by subway or taxi; twenty to thirty minutes on foot. Because Dolores never went out, the chances of us running into one another were unlikely. I simply stopped visiting or talking with her.

At first it was easy; I wondered why I hadn't previously tried this tactic. She left me messages, but I didn't return her calls. Then her friends telephoned.

"You should get in touch with your mother," one said.

"How can you call yourself a daughter?" another asked.

"Your behavior is disgraceful; you should be ashamed of yourself."

These admonitions were uttered by people enlisted by Dolores to administer a daily dose of guilt. She was their confidante, the woman who lit up their rooms and enthralled them with her stories, the one whom they looked at without question or apprehension. And they were women and men who made their livings without engaging in fraud or scams, mothers and fathers whose children spoke to them, I was sure, if not about their private lives, at least about their daily ones.

What had she told them? Surely she had neglected to mention the lies she had told Mr. Tell, an ordinary man in an ordinary suit, who had brought to light the criminal pursuits of Dolores Buxton, intricate schemes in which she had fashioned and juggled several personae, presaging what we now call identity theft.

I'm certain none of them knew that my mother perpetrated fraud using the social security numbers of the unsuspecting, often vulnerable women who rented the back room of her apartment. Because she collected disability, my mother was eligible for subsidized home health care. On paper she transformed those young women into home health-care attendants she had "hired," for whom she received money from a Medicare-funded agency (subsidy that was supposed to be used to pay them). She even convinced them—for a reduction in rent? Some cash? A promise to be included in the acknowledgments of the books she claimed to be writing?—to submit urine samples to be drug tested. What would Dolores's friends have thought of her had they known about her secret life and illegal activities?

The Easter Sunday in 1989 before my mother committed suicide, I went to Central Park with my friend Andrew. We walked under a bridge spanning the horse path. Ambling, let alone walking on a dirt road, was the kind of thing Dolores and I had never done together.

"If she and I went into therapy together," I suggested, "perhaps we could work things out."

"Maybe," he said.

I loved his way of wringing out a situation into one word. *Maybe.* The perhapsness of Dolores was exactly the right distillation of her essence. Andrew, who had been offered a full university scholarship at seventeen in computer science at Caltech, was good at reducing things to their smallest, most critical parts. He looked at the world and saw taxonomies and grammars of zeroes and ones that are invisible to most of us. Though he had never met Dolores, he recognized her criminal mind because he had once been a member of a famous computer-hacker gang in the early eighties when he was a teenager. And he was also, after my mother died, the only friend I entrusted with a set of keys to my apartment. He'd let himself in after the long graveyard shift he worked at a comic-book store in Brooklyn that was two hours away from where I lived. He'd wash his feet and quietly settle into bed, wrapping his arms around me until we both fell asleep. I had become afflicted, unsurprisingly, with insomnia. On the nights he came to my place, when I heard sleep in his breathing I'd touch his wrist, and the rhythm of his pulse helped me drift. Andrew died several years later, by drowning in the East River. The circumstances of his death were forever unknown. Suicide suspected by some. Murder by others.

But then, he was alive and well and living and we were, before Dolores ended her life, spending time together. Andrew and I discovered that we shared a certain disdain for therapists. It seemed, we thought, that almost anyone with a problem, time, or money, or, perhaps, that everyone with a problem *and* money in New York City was "in therapy," a phrase that stood in for a secret handshake. Andrew, who lived on a scant income in a sparsely furnished walk-up in Union Square, called the talking cure a waste of resources. And though I appreciated then and value now objective emotional counsel, as soon as I articulated the suggestion, I knew it was a ludicrous idea.

Who was I kidding to think therapy would untangle the Gordian knot of such a relationship? My mother had spent years manipulating doctors (including experienced analysts of all persuasions), using them to support her disability claims, and often outsmarting them to obtain prescriptions for narcotic drugs, which other physicians would not write because she had been reported to the Narcotics Register (active in New York City until 1974) as a suspected or known opiate user. The fact is this: she was an addict. It is likely that my father, who discovered syringes hidden in the closet of her hospital room the day after I was born, asked his physician brother to add her name to that official list.

The last time I visited Dolores, we watched television, which is how we spent time together when she mustered the energy to leave the back bedroom where she resided the last months of her life. I was one of only three people to see her in the habitual state in which she existed, outfitted in an old pink bathrobe, her hair pulled into a loose ponytail, no makeup highlighting what once was an innately show-stopping face on which no line, angle, or curve had been wasted and which had become a brittle mask. All disappointment was hers, I thought then.

"Why don't you get dressed and we'll go out to the store?" I said.

"My back hurts." She sighed. The blinds and curtains were drawn. How did she know if it was day or night?

Upon hearing me say *out*, her dog, a Yorkshire terrier named BG, rattled his crate in the kitchen. He knew that one-syllable word and listened for it with the attentiveness that consumes those who are deprived.

"I'll get the dog," I said.

The moment I unlatched the door to the small metal cage, BG nipped my heels, voiced his high-pitched yip, barked and growled, raced down the hall and back into the room where my mother sat. He charged at her slippered toes then completed another circuit, down the hall and back into the kitchen, where he yipped and snarled at me.

"Put the dog back in his crate," Dolores instructed from the other room.

"But he needs to go out," I said. BG whined.

"Kim, just take him. And when you get back, put him in the crate."

"Why don't you come with me?"

"No."

I wanted then to shake Dolores as if we were both in some made-for-TV movie in which I was her best friend, and she trusted me to tell her the unmitigated truth. I wanted to tell her how unfair it was to cage a sentient creature for almost twenty-four hours, to let it shrink in a loneliness I couldn't bear to witness, especially because like her, the dog had become unlikable, a creature I could neither offer to care for or comfort. My dislike for an animal I pitied shamed me; why didn't I take him, or, at the very least, advocate more ardently for him? As I receded from this responsibility, Dolores retreated more and more, relinquishing to others the responsibility of walking the dog. Several months before she died, my mother gave BG to a young man who lived in the neighborhood.

"We should have paid attention to *that*," one of her friends told me at the memorial service.

But we hadn't heeded the signs of my mother's letting go, first of herself, then the dog, then life. And I will remain forever unsure of what it might have meant to have noticed her slippage. The skeptic in me might tell you it wouldn't have mattered—she was determined to go her way. But the part of me interested in possibility wants to believe that in the company of empathy and love, pain might be softened.

On Easter Sunday 1989, my mother left me her final message, though I didn't realize I'd never hear her voice again: "Forgive her, she knows not what she does." *One more layer of hyperbole*, I thought, erasing the tape in that inattentive way I had fashioned to respond to Dolores's exaggeration. Comparing herself to Christ, what chutzpah! I never considered that the *her* in that recorded instruction might have referred not to my mother, but to me. That she was narrating this last piece

42

of our story as if I were the one who had nailed her to a cross, or, worse, because the tacit complicity of our relationship forced her to do unto herself what I could not do.

Therapy was clearly not an option.

Besides, what might I have told a therapist with my mother present: "I can't forgive you?" or "You're always lying"? Perpetually unable to confront Dolores, I was then equally incapable of admitting that I judged her for the pathological nature of her bad behavior. Now, with the perspective of time and the cliché but inevitable understanding of how I might have screwed up had I become a mother, I know she did the best she could, which meant she hadn't anticipated, and was unable to locate or develop in herself, the time and energy required to raise a child. Dolores liked to justify her shortcomings; the word *neglect* was absent when it came to telling our story, just as the words *unyielding pain* went unacknowledged in my account. By her account, she had survived one medical trauma after another as a young girl, a condition that caused her addiction to painkillers (the euphemism she used for heroin and, when she could no longer inject because of the excruciating cratered sores in her buttocks caused by the practice known as skin popping, any manner of opioid drug, from Talwin to Demerol). In her version of things, even if she did use painkillers, no one should forget that she had fought for custody of me and lost because the system was stacked against her; *she* was the victim. Were therapists to listen to her version of the story—how illness had disabled her and caused her chemical dependency; how my father won custody of me because of his legal and political connections; how she struggled as a single woman on welfare and was the target of multiple discriminations—they might have looked at me as if I, a relentlessly bitter and unforgiving daughter, needed psychodynamic intervention. A therapist could have easily ended up becoming Dolores's ally.

I knew how it worked because I had watched her manipulate my high-school boyfriends into believing her and questioning me; she knew a mark when she saw one, and adolescent males coming up in 1970s Manhattan didn't stand a chance against her alluring older-woman savoir faire, her Blanche DuBois charm and vulnerability, and her astonishing, though peeling-at-the-corners glamor. Once even I had believed her. In that fairytale ideal of Once Upon a Time—the legacy of so many generations of mothers inherited by so many generations of daughters—Dolores was still able to work her spell on me.

IV. "if the day is ending, or the world"

Three days after her forgive-her-she-knows-not message, I came home to find the answering machine's red light blinking twice. I resented the intrusion, thinking I might hear recordings of more biblical admonishments, words twisted to enrich the emotional petri dish in which Dolores was attempting to culture an impending sense of doom and guilt, a reading, perhaps, of some other scripture or doctrine, performed by one of my mother's friends. I tried to guess, but failed to imagine, which one of them would take on "Whither thou goest, I shall go," or "You've got to set thine house in order." I wanted to ignore the two messages. But something nagged at me to listen to them, something between curiosity—the sort you have passing the scene of an accident—and shame. There were, after all, times when I chastised myself for being a cruel and undeserving daughter in spite of the legal justifications to which I clung. The as-yet unformed and not-quite-responsible adult inside me knew my mother's mental health was deteriorating, and that spending more time with her might contribute to an atmosphere which promoted happiness, if not hers, then maybe ours. The kid I used to be had wanted to become Dolores's grown-up daughter, and somewhere in that imagined adulthood, I had seen myself as a self-possessed young woman who expressed gratitude for her mother's generosity and perseverance. But that child and the adult she would become were buried deep beneath the person I really

45

was in 1989, a young woman emerging from her twenties, that age of self-involvement in which, I believed, parents needed to be held at a distance.

I pushed the Play button.

"Kim, this is John," said a soft, Irish-accented voice, one I had not expected to hear. "Please call me." He pronounced the numerals with deliberation, as if he had deciphered a secret code accorded to their sequence. In the second message, which he left an hour later, his voice trembled. "I hate to do this—" he started. Then the sharp sound of a single breath, a hesitation that made me take note. "I hate to leave this message…but your mum's dead and you need to come home."

How much did she pay him? Even as that question surfaced, I knew it was an unbelievable first thought to entertain when you learn from a disembodied voice on an answering machine that your mother has died. And the word *home* vexed me; Dolores had spent most of her life pulling up stakes; the divorce from my father catalyzed six moves in as many years, ending with the apartment on West Seventieth Street. When my parents first separated, I was three. The court awarded custody initially to my mother. During those years I lived with her, she'd drop me off at a friend's or cousin's place. Sometimes for an entire week. On many occasions, she left me alone overnight. Often she stayed in bed all day and night and I simply didn't eat. Once, she handed me over to my father for fourteen months, declaring I had become unmanageable. It was then that Phoebe convinced my father to contest the custody decision.

Home is a loaded concept for just about anyone; for me, it is first fractured, then quiet, dark, or belongs to someone else and is thus foreign. Once I went to live with my father and stepmother, Phoebe, home became real enough, defined by their ability to provide me with an urban Jewish girl's modern life, complete with festive Rosh Hashanah dinners, Passover seders celebrated with Phoebe's relatives, menorahs kindled at Hanukah, a private-school education, a place "in the country" as New York City dwellers say, and traveling abroad. Though I embraced the culturally Jewish environment, I proclaimed myself at seventeen anti-bourgeois and rejected the privileges of such a life. (Picture that adolescent for just a minute: she is so sure of her opinions, but she is also a girl who likes to read and can spend hours drawing patterns and whose standing wish, one of the few memories she has of an enduring desire, is to live on the beach in a shack with a horse.) Now I see the home that *didn't* happen—a mother and daughter learning about one another in an environment in which both thrive—and how it is, still, charged with sentimentality and the particulate matter of wanting to return. But to *where?* I must always ask myself once such nostalgia overtakes me.

As I listened to John's message, I thought of all those places we had called home, Dolores and I, summoning elements from each in a series of memory fragments that matched the moves my mother had made from one part of the city to another with me in tow: a Dionne Warwick album on a yellow bedspread; a painted-white, brick exterior; a grocery list removed from a patent-leather pocketbook and left on the Formica-topped kitchen table; how the light of late afternoon fell and then faded on black-and-white linoleum-tiled floors.

And then I pictured John, the porter in the co-op my mother's building had become, a young Irish fellow who had immigrated to America to make a life. A man who went to Mass on Sundays with his wife and infant son. Whom my mother paid to run the errands she had stopped running by herself—grocery shopping, walking the dog, retrieving and posting mail. He went outdoors in her stead, fetched and lifted, administering the quotidian tasks that connect us to the passing hours of any given day, rituals that join us to one another in a loop of community stitched of seemingly mundane yet essential threads. John was the sort of fellow who brought back the correct change and opened the mailbox door twice to make sure the envelopes had slid down the chute. He could not be lying.

I dialed his number.

"Your mum's dead," he told me.

"I'll be there right away," I said. But despite the choked-back sadness in John's voice, despite everything I knew about him that told me he was telling the truth, that he *couldn't* tell this sort of lie, I refused to believe that my mother was actually dead, as if in *this* story, Dolores had defied death itself, proving once and for all to her now disbelieving daughter that all along she had been honest.

V. *"You think of how your hair looks / I think of the ends of things"*

I changed my clothes and called Andrew, who didn't answer. "If you don't hear from me later," I said, leaving a message, "please check to see if I've been arrested." I was convinced my mother had somehow convinced John to call me and say she was dead, that she was in trouble with someone, somewhere, and had managed to implicate me in her scams, and, once I arrived at her apartment, the police were going to whisk me off to jail.

Who is completely innocent, after all? Several years earlier, I had helped my mother with one of her schemes. I participated by pretending to be one of the fictional home-care aides created with the identities of young women who had rented the back room of her apartment. One of them had just moved out, and my mother needed someone to submit a urine sample so she could collect the paycheck. I peed in a cup under a false name. Afterward, I threw up.

"You can't count on me anymore to help you," I told her.

She was furious. I had been staying with her then, trying to land upright after three years of living abroad, studying applied linguistics in a town tucked into the mountains in eastern France, traveling through southern Spain and northern Africa, and living and working on a dairy farm in the Pyrenees Mountains. My return to the States in the early fall of 1987 was unremarkable: I was broke, sick with a severe case of intestinal parasites, uninsured, unemployed, and single. I spoke fluent French and some Spanish, had read Balzac, Voltaire, and Hugo, but entertained few prospects for my own writing. I ignored all that and called myself a poet, but really all I was doing was archiving impressions of people, places, and things, collecting experiences, moving from the vast restlessness I experienced at twenty-seven to a vaster recklessness I practiced at twenty-eight. Dolores suggested I come home, and I accepted her invitation; what kid, even one who is closer to thirty years old, says no to a large room on West Seventieth Street in a large apartment with cable TV and a stocked refrigerator? I'd like to believe that such shallowness did not define me, but in retrospect, I see I was easily lured. Within a few weeks, however, I grew weary of her self-imposed gloom—the permanently drawn shades and curtains, the suicidal declarations over breakfast, how she stood silently in the doorway of my bedroom, watching me as I transcribed into type my handwritten poems. Then came the pee-in-a-cup incident, after which we moved about the apartment in a silence statically charged with a subterranean hostility. By maintaining different schedules, we avoided one another in the hallway and the kitchen. I saved money from waiting tables and moved out in October.

It didn't occur to me that Dolores's need to shape identity—by theft, with lies, through a variety of invented narratives—was her vocation. Nor did I want to fully parse out and examine "the plain and simple fact" as my father put it, that my mother (his fourth wife), if faced with the choice of lying or telling the truth, chose to lie. I couldn't fathom that Dolores, whose confidence-man father used her to assist him in the performance of various crimes and misdemeanors, was merely authoring her life in all the ways a writer might fashion a novel or a painter might make a portrait. What if that's the only way Dolores knew how to live, in an extravagant artifice whose very origins had become, because of how painful they were, invisible even to her?

The taxi pulled up to her building where a police cruiser was parked, conspicuously, it seemed, in accordance with what I had imagined as my mother's plan. Obviously, though not to me at the time, if someone had wanted to arrest me, they wouldn't have provided an opportunity for me to turn around from a potential crime scene and flee.

For an instant, I wondered if the cab driver was part of this whole scenario. Could he hear my heart pounding? He turned and looked at me.

"I have to tell you something," he said.

I pretended to be distracted while rummaging in my bag for the fare, an excuse to not look up and make eye contact, which would surely implicate me (this is why I don't play poker). My breath almost stopped right then, and I felt lightheaded until my mouth opened to gasp (*of its own accord*, I later thought). Surely in the next minute, he was going to tell me he was an undercover cop.

"You are very beautiful," he said.

I collected myself as best I could, starting with an internal admonishment to separate what is imagined from what is real.

"You should see my mother—she's the real thing," I said, in one of those rare moments possessed of *l'esprit de l'escalier,* the wit you need—and often despair of not having—when witless things, said in ignorance or out of intolerance, or even, as in that moment, with sincerity, are spoken. I tendered a five-dollar bill, pushed open the door, and stepped out of the vehicle.

The elevator in my mother's building was always sluggish, but on March 29, 1989, it ascended to the fourth floor so slowly that I had time to think about what it meant to grow up as a mere shadow, or aftermath, of great beauty, one that goes wrong and must, as Keats says, die. During the 1960s, when I was still under the age of ten and Dolores in her thirties, she wore her long, straight platinum-blonde hair parted down the middle. Tall and slender, her breasts often braless, her voice evoking Lauren Bacall, she had cultivated by the start of the 1970s a retrofitted version of a femme fatale descended from the noir canon of the fifties. When she went out—for family gatherings, on a date, to the store, for a meal—she wore headbands, false eyelashes, bright pink or red lipstick, and tight, short skirts and dresses. Over time she morphed into a cliché—once the aspiring ingénue, she became a version of the aging but formerly glamorous movie star sequestered in her home, bitter and unable to alter the tragic fate of being alone. Dolores never had a screen or stage career, but anyone who has ever met or seen pictures of her thought she should have been an actress. Which, of course, she had become, though her stage was private, her scenes enacted in exchange for attention, and the players able and likely to bleed, from wounds inflicted both to the literal flesh and the figurative heart.

As the elevator reached the third floor, I recalled, too, what my relationship with my mother had resembled during the last two months of no contact: the daily phone calls at work that ended with me slamming down the receiver and the feeling I might wake up one morning with my identity erased, trapped as a pretend character my mother wanted me to play in her real-life dramas. As the elevator inched upward, nearing the fourth floor but not quite there, I imagined myself in court, my head turned toward the jury, explaining that to live in Dolores's apartment, I was obliged—under threat of psychic excommunication—to follow her rules and orders. I had learned as a child to fear at all costs anything that might lead to separation from my mother. I regretted not having thought of therapy earlier; if an analyst had been familiar with this narrative, I would now have a qualified expert to testify on my behalf, to tell the judge and jury how completely sick and deranged Dolores Buxton really was, how complex her machinations, how binding her emotional blackmail. After all, this was a woman who, before she met and married my father in 1958, had been indicted on assault charges. A woman who claimed she had been engaged to G. David Shine and who referred to Bob Hope as a "close friend." And she was also a woman—a "shapely blonde," the newspapers, in write-ups about her alleged violent crime, had called her, though the reporters neglected to paint for readers how she possessed everyone's attention the minute she entered a room.

VI. "And the face once this surface knew / Stirs no such shadows any more."

The elevator stopped, and the door opened. Two paramedics stood on the landing. *How could Dolores do this?* I thought. *How could she assemble so many willing actors to play out scenes contrived for me and me alone?* During brief intervals, I was able to see myself from a remove, and in those instances I knew my thinking was irrational. I gave into it anyway; with my mother, anything was possible. She had, after all, ignored the doctors who warned her not to have children, birthing me in spite of the danger to herself. At least that was one page from the Cliff Notes for the Legend of Dolores Buxton, a narrative she fed me as a child, through my adolescence, and into my young adulthood. *How much did she pay these people? Where was she hiding that kind of money?* Maybe she hadn't told me about all her schemes and was quite wealthy. Perhaps I didn't know her as well as I thought (of course I didn't know her, I think now—who really *knows* their living parents?). I nodded to the paramedics and entered the apartment.

John sat on the living-room sofa with Leonardo, the on-site superintendent of the building, a man who had tended to my mother for over fifteen years. He lived in a first-floor apartment with his wife and three Chihuahuas, the kind of dogs my mother had when she was younger, dogs she stopped to pet on those rare days when she went out. And Dolores was something to see when she left the apartment.

This was a woman who didn't simply dress; she spent hours preparing for any excursion, commonplace or formal. One summer afternoon in the early 1980s still startles me with its vivid, cinematic quality. I had agreed to accompany her to the Food Emporium, an outing for which I dressed in jeans and a T-shirt. She wore a straw hat and a lemon-yellow linen suit with lime accents on the sleeves. Her purse, gloves, and shoes were variations on the theme of orange. She was the only person I've ever known who went to the grocery store outfitted as if she were a celebrity who might suddenly have to sign autographs or grant an interview.

We ambled down Columbus Avenue: her light-blonde hair tucked beneath the hat's brim, the citrus of her clothing, the yellow-white of her hair, and paleness of her skin suggested sunflowers and lemonade on a porch far away, in a place where folks still left doors unlocked. She carried such a juxtaposition of geographies—a breath of Great-Lakes-rural air, rife with petals and corn, against the thick, humid scent of asphalt that has baked in the white sun of a hot summer day. In the dust and turmoil of Manhattan's anonymity and dirt, when she went out, my mother was that call to life that saves a city street from itself.

The truth: when I was younger, such fanfare and color coordination mortified me; everything she did seemed overdone. The bleachiness of Dolores made me uneasy: the whitening she practiced seemed an accusation of shadows, darkness, and of my own Semitic proclivities of nose and complexion. Unable to dress or walk or converse as she did, I did not possess her elegance, that mature grace earned by women who came of age in the forties and fifties, women who knew how to wear pencil skirts, show a bit of leg, fasten millinery to their hair with hatpins. But there was,

56

too, a rigidity to her faithful and formal rendering of herself, and when I was in my teens and twenties, like most young people who need to contradict the adults in their lives, I resented what I saw as my mother's unstoppable pretense. And now here I am, amazed by her make-believe, for what it says about the perseverance of her imagination.

I was seven mnth's shy of thirty at the end of March 1989, the same age as Dolores when she defied the gravity of medical opinion and delivered me into the world. Standing in her apartment, where she had spent most of the time these last years in bed, with windows covered and lights dimmed, I didn't—couldn't—believe she had died. John and Leonardo sat on the couch, both leaning at a forward angle, heads resting in their respective hands. They seemed suspended in their identical postures, as if the solemnity of how they were bent was part of the script Dolores had written. Two policemen greeted me, and their presence chipped at my disbelief that my mother was, truly, dead. Yet somehow I still entertained the possibility that these uniformed men would be escorting *me* out of the apartment and "down to the station" as they say in all the television crime shows.

Instead, the officers told John and Leonardo they were free to go.

"I'm so sorry, Kim," Leonardo said as he stood, looking at the floor.

John's eyes were red, his face pale. He had discovered Dolores's dead body earlier, when he came up with the mail, and she hadn't answered him. But I hadn't yet seen how she looked when he found her.

"It's a crying shame," he said, the airy lilt of his voice lending brief respite to that somber moment.

He shook his head. Did he know I hadn't spoken to Dolores in two months? His tone concealed any opinion he might have had or whether he thought it a shame because the woman in apartment 4A was dead at fifty-nine or because her only child had abandoned her. Had she informed him of my absence in this, her time of great need? Had she told him I lived nearby? Perhaps Dolores, a faded beauty but a beauty nonetheless, had been kind to him in ways I had never experienced. Certainly he could not imagine a mother withholding such kindnesses from her own child. Shame, which often manifests as a rush of warmth surging in the face, is a tireless dance of uncovering and covering.

After John and Leonardo left, the policemen followed me into the kitchen, which suddenly felt too small, appointed with furnishings and appliances that seemed too large. These two cops appeared enormous, and I would have sworn that they had to duck to enter the room, as if the furniture—which looked as if it belonged in a kindergarten classroom—could not accommodate their girth or heft. I smelled the metal of their guns and shields, the blue in their uniforms, the grime on their once-polished, now-scuffed shoes. I saw the scratches in the leather of their belts and the frayed cotton on their shoelaces, and in those small and relatively unapparent markings of daily wear and tear were all the tragedies these two men had seen, including today's misfortune, which they were describing as a potential suicide. We stood in the kitchen, where my mother had sat every day at noon to eat her first meal of the day, half a Lender's onion bagel lightly buttered and one cup of decaf coffee sweetened with half a packet of Equal. They informed me what would happen next, but I heard only the most obvious words: *unattended death* and *coroner*. If they hadn't suggested we go to my mother's bedroom, the kitchen, decorated only a year ago in black and white with red accents, would have started spiraling in a cartoonish vortex.

The walk down the hallway to her bedroom seemed to take longer than the ride in the elevator, which I might have sworn had occurred a full year before this moment, which stretched beyond the future or memory. As we left the kitchen, my dread of being arrested started to wear off, and a different sensation—one of cold firmness that anchored me to the carpet and weighted my feet—began to erode the denial that my mother was dead. *It's possible she's really gone*, I thought, placing one foot in front of the other in what felt like an accelerated tempo, moving along a hall I had walked thousands of times over the course of two decades and was now traveling with two larger-than-life policemen at my side.

The bedroom door was ajar. One of the cops said something in a low voice—what exactly I cannot recall—something he had been trained to say, at a time such as this, or, perhaps, to ease me into the room. He pushed the door open. Dolores's naked body was stretched out on the bed, her eyes wide open, her mouth stretched into the kind of expression you expect on the face of a drowning person.

I entered the room and my vision sharpened. *This is how crows might see*, I thought. In elegant acuity, the things I beheld just then seemed to vibrate, as if they were breathing. Dominating the silver perfume tray was a large, unopened bottle of Chanel No. 5, whose soft, square corners were, even at this strange juncture of worry and discovery, free of dust. The label was slightly yellowed, and I wondered why my mother had never used that perfume. *Such a waste*, I thought. A set of keys fanned out on the dresser, their metal teeth raised above the marble top where whorls of gray eddied slowly under the objects on its surface, including two photographs of me in pewter frames.

These were the last things my mother looked at before she died, or at least they were the last earthly things she saw before seeing whatever had caused the terrified, stretched O of her mouth now contorting her face. On the night table next to where she lay was a glass of water, drained but for a sip, an emptied vial of digoxin with the instructions to "take one tablet as needed," and a piece of paper torn out of a spiral notebook and folded, its blue horizontal lines and red vertical margin electric in the low light of the north-facing bedroom. The drapes had been opened, which surprised me. Had she sought to cast a natural light on her body, to make plain the many scars and wounds sustained by her flesh? On the floor, a pair of pink house mules—*when had she worn them last?* I wondered—pointed out from the bed as though Dolores had planned to slip her feet into them during the night if she rose to use the bathroom or have a snack. A gilt-framed, overly sentimental painting of a little girl in a field of flowers hung, slightly crooked, over the bed. My mother had stolen the picture from the Copley Plaza in Boston when I lived in Cambridge in the late 1970s and she had come to visit me. On the rose print of the pillowcase, a stain of faint yellow saliva that had dribbled from her mouth as she died.

"Why has no one bothered to shut her eyes?" I asked in a voice so inconsequential that neither of the officers heard me, or if they did, they chose to ignore my question. *Six people have come into this room before me. Why is she lying there exposed?* I must have looked as if I were about to collapse because one of the policemen reached out to hold my arm and asked if I'd be okay.

The question was impossible to answer honestly. I was not okay taking in the image of my mother's exposed body. I was not okay navigating the simultaneous relief and despair of this death.

"We need to have a look through things," one of the cops said. "Standard procedure. We'll need to remove any cash or valuables."

At that announcement, I flushed. The objects in the room that had seemed so alive in the light of shock-induced clearsightedness became once again perfume bottles, keys, and photographs caught in the panicked gaze of a woman about to take her last breath. I sensed Dolores's fear just then, as if it were stale air seeping into the room through the cracks between the molding and the floor. And with each inhalation, I absorbed these particles of fright until they coalesced, quickening my heartbeat and making me perspire just enough to smell my own sweaty angst. The jewelry my mother had reported stolen as part of her fraudulent insurance claim was, of course, somewhere in this room. One of the men opened the dresser. The two top right drawers were filled with undergarments, each piece folded and arranged in neat piles according to color and size. *Please don't touch my mother's lingerie, don't put your large cop hands on those articles that were once close to her skin,* I silently implored, in a strange and almost childish moment of sympathy for my mother's privacy. He closed the drawer. *Don't waste your wishes on her underwear,* I cautioned myself, *wait till they get to the jewelry boxes.* The officer opened the next drawer—filled with her brassieres—and just as quickly closed it. Then the one containing her gloves—lace, cotton, velvet, leather, kid—in plastic bags, organized according to length, color, and fabric. As he opened each remaining drawer, his eyes scanned the pantyhose, scarves, and sweaters. "Nothing here," he announced.

Really? I thought for an instant. Didn't they see the obsessive-compulsive *order* in those drawers, the just-so arrangement of everything, as if Dolores knew all along that they'd be coming today and inspecting her belongings? Did they not, as I did, if even for the briefest of moments (and in spite of the earlier impulse to protect her undergarments from their scrutiny), want to mess things up, rummage through the panties and bras and all those other accessories? Weren't they, as fellow human beings, curious; didn't they want to find something, if not evidence of a crime, some clue that explained the naked, dead woman in the room?

The other policeman examined the jewelry boxes. I watched him, but tried to look as if I were staring past the wall, hoping I appeared possessed of a grief-stricken expression appropriate for a daughter seeing her dead, naked mother for the first time. The officer opened one box after another. First, the rings: An aquamarine set in platinum, a ruby in white gold, emeralds and diamonds embedded in yellow gold, pearl and sapphire raised on rose-gold prongs, a gold knot. Then the flash of a pearl-and-emerald brooch that had been a gift from my father, an antique lorgnette my mother wore around her neck and used to read poetry when she received visitors, and a variety of bracelets that once graced her wrists. All pieces that Dolores claimed had been stolen. I held my breath. Mr. Tell, I thought without really wanting to think about him, would have been smugly pleased to discover, finally, the truth of the claim he was investigating.

"Nothing but costume jewelry here," the officer informed his partner.

I wasn't going to argue with him. Blood rushed to my head. By some extraordinary fortune, I had been spared. Though I sensed that my luck was temporary, and that no one is spared in the aftermath of suicide.

We left the bedroom. The coroner's office, one of the policemen explained, would send someone to retrieve my mother's body and transport it to the morgue. He asked for the original Last Will and Testament, which I located and handed over. He advised me not to remove anything from the apartment. When a will hasn't been probated or an inventory made, he explained, an estate has to remain intact.

"We're done here, Miss," he said. "I'm sorry for your loss." And just as quickly as they had arrived, they departed.

VII: *"Her bare // Feet seem to be saying: / We have come so far, it is over."*

I called my best friend. As I waited for her, I phoned the priest of a local church, smoked and paced in the living room, avoided the kitchen and the hallway. When Roberta arrived, we went into my mother's bedroom. I was struck then by Dolores's swollen feet, so I knelt on the floor and rubbed them.

"What are you doing?" Roberta asked.

"You should rub the feet of the dead so they can walk comfortably to where they need to go," I said. As if I *knew* this was so, as if I weren't cobbling together a ritual and its meaning in order to prove I had faith in something other than the increasing sensation that I was the one who needed to be forgiven. Dolores expected me to feel guilt, and to subsequently wonder what I might have done to exonerate myself from being the daughter who had caused her mother such deep pain that she would end her own life. "Forgive her," she had asked. A quarter of a century passed before I was able to actively imagine the loneliness and despair she inhabited, though I've never come close to what must have been the deadening endlessness of days and nights that she certainly experienced, a life lived on an edge that must have been as sheer as any real precipice. I suspect she was asking my future self to forgive who I was then. I didn't know that I didn't know what I had done.

But I also wanted to relieve that swelling in her ankles and toes, an obscene reminder of my mother's pain, which she had talked about persistently and was a condition I thought she overplayed. Maybe rubbing her feet was the final performance of an act I had rehearsed throughout my childhood every other Saturday night, after she had lost custody of me and I visited her, when she convinced me to love her without hesitation, staying up late to watch old horror movies and "pulling her toes" as she called stretching the fabric of the pantyhose that constricted her feet. Perhaps it was the guilt I was supposed to feel that needed to be rubbed away. Her heels were cool, the insteps stiff, and, pressing into those feet, I was vaguely aware that this was the last time I would touch my mother's body.

Roberta removed the necklace Dolores wore, a tiny pendant on a delicate gold chain that lay between her breasts. On one side of the charm was a Star of David; on the other a simple cross. I didn't think to ask which side was facing up but later wished I had. The idea that faith has sides nagged at me for years afterward. I wondered which side my mother had chosen, or if some involuntary muscular twitch had decided things for Dolores. What heaven or hell or purgatory, what world to come do you enter when the key you wear around your neck, the symbol of your beliefs, opens more than one door?

And which system of belief might assuage what was rapidly coalescing into a feeling of guilt? I was the daughter who had gone absent. I was the one who had asked, after my mother repeatedly pronounced how depressed she was and how she wanted to end her life, "What do you have to be depressed about?" while simultaneously thinking, *Go ahead, end it all, do whatever you need to do.*

Roberta clasped the necklace around my neck. She hugged me good-bye and left. I covered my mother's body with the sheet and opened the piece of notebook paper from the night table. It didn't occur to me then that the police never picked up or looked at this note, at least not while I was in the room with them. At an unattended death with no suspicion of homicide, they call the coroner, who in turn determines the cause of death.

I read what she had written, her last words:

Dearest Kim:

If you receive this either I'll be gone or in the hospital. Sorry, I couldn't stand all the pain.

I've written out things you should know. I hope you'll follow up.

There is a small manila envelope on side of my bed.

Sorry, we couldn't spend our last few months together.

That comma after the word *sorry* was such a dramatic pause after so succinct an apology. Then there was her use of the collective possessive pronoun in the last line, "*Our* last few months," as if she thought *I* would be dying soon (perishing from the remorse I was sure to feel). I couldn't believe she hadn't signed the note. My mother had always made a point of signing everything, from forgeries of author inscriptions and signatures in books, to her own ideas for projects— cosmetic products, film scripts, business ventures—jotted on cocktail napkins, in the margins of spiral-bound notebooks, and on errant pieces of paper bound together with thin rubber bands into tight little packages stored in drawers throughout the apartment. But not *this* note, which made it seem as if she had already killed the self who believed in all the stories she had invented. I reached along the side of the bed and found the envelope with the longer, more detailed letter.

Before I could read it, the buzzer rang. I opened the door to Father Fred Balinong, a compactly muscular man with a buzz cut. Just enough smile tempered his earnest somberness, introducing the possibility of humanity into what was, decidedly, a pretty grim and chaotic scene. As I brought him down the hallway to the bedroom, I began to feel like a tour guide in a surreal version of *This Is Your Life*, that only-in-1950s-America reality-documentary television show, which ended in 1961, was revived a decade later, and reprised briefly in the 1980s. Maybe I watched an episode with my mother, maybe even a rerun she had seen when it first aired. Dolores was just starting to date my father when Frances Farmer, the actress kept against her will in a psychiatric hospital for eight years, appeared on the show in 1958. "If someone is treated like a patient, they're likely to act like one," she had commented.

"I lost my own mother twelve years ago," the priest said, interrupting the tangent my mind had taken. "One continues to ache."

But my temples were not throbbing; my stomach was not lurching; my heart was not pounding. Instead, a numbness had started to wrap itself around me like a damp chill, one from which I was not going to emerge for more than a decade. It was as if some interior self, in an attempt to hide this event from my consciousness, had taken over the whole show. *You can't know this now*, it intimated.

Father Fred Balinong sat on the edge of the bed. After he closed Dolores's eyes, his hand lingered for an instant, and the gesture yanked me out of the as-yet-flimsy cocoon of detachment and made me yearn for all the gentleness that had been denied to Dolores throughout her life. I explained to him that although my mother was half Jewish, I wanted to honor my Catholic grandmother and great-grandmother by holding the memorial in a church.

"She killed herself," I said, as if confessing on her behalf. He looked at me without blinking and administered last rites.

As he enunciated the Latin words, I heard echoes of the message she had left on my answering machine on Easter Sunday: *Forgive her, she knows not what she does.* If it's true that she was asking that *I* be forgiven, such forgiveness depended on me growing up, casting aside the sticky envelope of chrysalis, and emerging to feel the loss in all the ways it was going to shake me. But what if she was asking me to forgive the part of her in myself she knew I was surely going to recognize once I matured? "What has been lost, and was found, is saved from being lost again," writes St. Augustine. But forgiveness turns out to be trickier than the simple act of losing and finding; instead, it must be fashioned, a little like a golem, with urgency, solemnity, the dignity of sacred words, and a willingness to undo what one has made with mud and breath.

The priest listened to the articulation of my wishes, his body canted toward mine as I spoke. He agreed to perform the service.

"What is your mother's name?" he asked.

"Dolores," I said, grateful for the present tense of his question.

He looked me in the eye. "Ah, yes," he said. "Dolores means *sorrows.*"

After Father Balinong left, I waited. Hours passed before the coroner arrived. Plenty of time to call people who needed to know that my mother was dead. Plenty of time to make arrangements. While the business of death is a surreal dance of consumerism disguised as a kind of distraction psychology, the act of making arrangements allows you to focus on everything but grief, at least until you wake up the next morning. I had already participated, with my father, in what I came to think of as grotesqueries six years earlier when Phoebe had died. But for Dolores's death, I was riding solo, telephoning the funeral home and talking about cremation options, calling the *New York Times* to inquire about rates and deadlines for obituaries.

My mother's death notice was short, mostly because obits are expensive. There were many things I might have written: that she could have been a painter had she made different decisions; or that she believed marriage should be difficult and divorce easy; that she called *Time* the magazine for people who can't read and *Newsweek* the one for people who can't think; or that she always won when she played Trivial Pursuit and was hard to beat at backgammon or Scrabble.

There was, too, the more involved, unpublishable-in-the-newspaper obituary—an elegy, really—which required decades to write, and which depicts Dolores as a woman who, in the simplest terms, left her mother's home in Rochester, New York, in search of another life, a path taken that resulted, ultimately, in making me and killing her. One might say, even, that the act of making me did, in fact, kill her.

And because that story was not one I was capable of telling and, too, because I didn't have the money to be wordy in a print obit, I stuck to the facts—the date she died, the day, place, and time of the memorial—omitting from the newspaper record not only the ways of her life, but also the true causes and nature of her dying, which had started years and years before she swallowed all those digoxin tablets.

My father was not included on my mother's list of people to telephone, but he was the first family member I called. Though my parents had barely spoken to one another outside a courtroom during the past twenty-five years, I figured my dad might want to know he had survived the fourth of his six wives.

"I'm sorry, sweetheart," he said. Maybe I heard just then a hint of relief in his voice, relief that it was she, not him, who had died first, leaving him to possess the only version of their failed-marriage story now that Dolores was dead. Perhaps I wanted to imagine him feeling that way so that he might later be justified in believing he was not responsible for contributing to his ex-wife's undoing.

Dwelling on my father's feelings was impossible when there were numbers to dial and decisions to make, and besides, Abner J. Kupperman was not a man who examined his emotional states in front of other people, even close kin. We said good-bye and both of us quietly and carefully returned our respective handsets to their receivers, a ritual we practiced for many years afterward, as if our leave-taking of one another was the first, never to be punctuated with a loud or clumsy hanging up. Then I called friends of my mothers, cousins, men who had loved her romantically and who had then backed into more platonic relationships. I called my half brothers, Ron and Ken, my stepbrother Gil, and my close friends.

"No," I told them all, "I don't know the exact time of the service yet. There'll be an obit in the *Times*; it'll say there."

I drank wine and smoked cigarettes. I talked with old friends who had known my mother. No tears fell from my eyes; nothing made me double over; my heart did not feel broken. Those responses came later—as I walked into the church for the memorial, in the middle of the night two months later, and at random moments ever after. There in the apartment where she died, her body still stretched out on the bed, I allowed myself the protection of the rote dialing, the repeated phrases I offered to those I called—"Sorry to be the bearer of bad news" and "My mother passed away this morning"—and the agitated waiting whose abrasive silences between conversations and seemingly endless emptiness I filled with Chardonnay and Marlboro Lights. Underneath it all, I felt relieved that the strain of our relationship was over, the screening of calls, the lectures from her friends, the tedious bureaucracy inherent in a refusal by a daughter to see or talk with her mother.

Several hours passed before the two technicians from the coroner's office arrived. How many miles had I paced before they came, meandering through the living room, kitchen, hallway, and bathroom, each room seeming more and more like a theatrical set, my movement more and more staged, my waiting more and more a rehearsal for the anticlimactic ringing of the doorbell? With the hurry-up-and-wait speed and latex-glove decorum of city mortuary employees, they handed me papers to sign, zipped my mother into a body bag, and removed her from the apartment, carrying her into the elevator and downstairs, downtown to the morgue, and down again to that building's basement. *Obitus*: a going down. *My mother in descent*, I thought, invoking a mixture of archetypal images that included Inanna undressing at each strata of the underworld; Eurydice at the precise moment that she wondered if Orpheus would turn his head and look back, Persephone, the Queen of the Shades, emerging above ground at spring.

Dolores: I was not ready to internalize what it meant to behold the last of her, or to become the last of her beheld when she died. After those two men carried my mother out and down, I turned off all the lights in the apartment and locked the door, and with these small gestures of pushing switches and turning keys, completed the act we call leaving home.

VIII. *"uprooting the [...] / dark cabbage of a heart?"*

"Would you like an autopsy performed?" asked the man from the coroner's office. We were talking on the phone; I was uptown and he was downtown at the morgue, in a building I expected then to visit but hadn't yet stepped foot in. For a moment, the several miles of city separating us—all that concrete, brick, steel, glass; the subterranean cacophony of wires, rails, pipes; and the mass of flora and fauna above and below ground—seemed to collapse, and for all I knew, he could have been on the other side of the wall.

"Certainly," I replied, my throat dry. He hung up; I stared blankly at the receiver in my hand before replacing it in the cradle. The sense I had of space contracting and expanding was not going to dissipate. If I remained still and listened hard enough, perhaps the scratch of a Bic ballpoint would be audible, somewhere in the New York City morgue, signing the authorization to dissect my mother's body.

When the man from the coroner's officer asked me about performing an autopsy, I knew my mother had bequeathed her body to science. But I did not know she had neglected to complete the hospital paperwork, which rendered moot her bequest. Nor did I know that autopsied bodies are not acceptable for medical donation; you don't just *leave* your body to science, as if Science were some gentleman, the kind who leaves calling cards and wears cravats and who salvages your corpse, no questions asked. I needed substantiation of her suicide, and the only way I was going to know for sure was if someone opened her body, poked needles into her veins, weighed and examined her organs.

My mother's lawyer, a man I preferred speaking with on the phone because of his terrible breath and bad comb-over, read me the riot act when he heard I had requested an autopsy.

"Medical donation was one of your mother's last wishes," he sputtered.

"But she hadn't—"

"There's no excuse. You are a selfish, self-centered girl. Your mother wanted to donate her body to science. What gives you the right to have decided otherwise?"

I hung up.

But he was right about one thing: I *was* selfish. I needed answers, wanted firm ground to stand on while the unreality of Dolores's suicide floated under and around my feet, threatening to divest me of the solidity of standing on firm ground. Because she had killed herself, an act that implied my mother was not of sound mind (and because I was her only next of kin), I was inclined to make—in fact, I felt righteous about making—any decisions I wanted about the corporeal Dolores who remained. Not only that, but I was already beginning to interpret my mother's death as an event that was happening not to *her*, but to *me*. In spite of all the mistakes she had made as a parent, she had provided me with my first home, the watery one inside her. When her body was gone, that home vanished. And the apartment in which she took her life was the last remnant of what has mostly disappeared for contemporary urban folk, a childhood home. I was not going to live there after the suicide; as it was, I could barely go back to her bedroom during the hours, days, and even weeks following her death. While I resist the tired adage "you can never go home," I also acknowledged it just then as a truth I couldn't escape.

When people, most of whom barely knew her, placed a hand on my shoulder and said, in those low, velvet tones reserved for the grieving, "So sorry for your loss," the phrase barely registered. On the continuum of relationship with my mother, I knew, even as it was occurring, that I had *gained* a new experience. Before her body was cremated, the ashes scattered, and all physical trace of my mother vanished, I knew that the weight of her choice to stop living would shape-shift with constancy.

My mother and I had never discussed her last wishes, unlike my father, who, during the last fifteen years of his life, managed to review his will and final arrangements with me at least once a month, then every week as he neared his end. I had no idea what my mother thought dying *was*, or if she believed (but just didn't care) that she'd end up in hell as a result of taking her own life. Similarly, she had no clue what her daughter might require in order to feel comforted (though both her short suicide note and the longer letter she composed imply that her choice to stop suffering might console me). These matters simply never came up in conversation, proving that in spite of close to thirty years of existing in a mother-daughter conundrum more often than not fraught with high-voltage tension, we were, in many ways, complete strangers.

What we believe and what we are often seem unbridged. How does a woman, brought up in two faiths that deem suicide a sin, decide to enact such an exit? Especially because

Dolores had, as a young child, been carried and cared for by the hands of grandparents and aunts and uncles who had fingered tefillin and pages of the Torah and who made gefilte fish and matzoh balls, *and* by those belonging to another set of grandparents, who had gone to church, said the rosary, spoke in sign language taught them by Catholic nuns, and would have told you firmly that you were wrong to not admit Christ, messiah and savior, into your heart. These were not merely sets of hands, but men and women, whom Dolores said she revered, missed, and, in the case of her mother, claimed she tried to save.

Beauty believes in itself and its duplication, and it was in service to beauty that my mother lived, paying for it with the destruction of her own. This cutting off the nose to spite the face, a kind of self-revenge, is a common-enough equation in Western culture, especially urban Western culture: beauty, when we worship it, can destroy us. But where does such turned-inside violence originate in the self? What must happen to switch off a belief engendered in faith, to end a life you did not create but which you were responsible for making into something other than what it became? In the absence of terminal illness, even the thought of the taking your own life requires despair of great vastness, obstacles that cannot be surmounted, a complete erasure of hope. Faith becomes conditional: *if there were a savior, I wouldn't feel so desperate; if God were tangibly real, we would not suffer so.* Or it devolves into a fierce belief in selfishness, cynicism, which is disbelief in human good, faith turned inside-out.

In June of 1989, I went to the Manhattan Mortuary to retrieve a report, prepared by Dr. Aglae Charlot, the associate medical examiner who conducted Dolores's autopsy. The report is a record of my mother's body just after she ended the life that once animated it. For example, her brain: it weighed 1300 grams and showed no signs of old or recent injuries, though inside that almost-three-pound organ resided the memory of pain and the aftermath of hurt, and the consciousness of a woman who had lost many of the things—pride, beauty, glamor, success—which she thought she was supposed to not only value but pursue with the fervor of a terrier in pursuit of a squirrel. Her lungs, 600 and 540 grams respectively, were both moderately congested, the result of smoking unfiltered Chesterfields and then Virginia Slims, cigarettes being, in her era, the de rigueur accessory of the modern, urban American woman. Her heart, weighing in at 340 grams—a scant three quarters of a pound, or the weight of a little blue heron—showed a "flabby consistency." Her body was that of a woman who had maintained a sedentary life. A woman who stopped her own heart with some pills, washed down with water. A woman who did not drink or exercise or hydrate or socialize or eat beyond the ritual of having to nourish oneself. A woman whose brain and heart together weighed a little over three and a half pounds, a weight that seems so insubstantial for such a larger-than-life woman.

Scars detected during the examination tell other stories about my mother's body: That she had had a facelift. Silicone breast implants. A C-section when I was born. A stomach operation. Three significant scars of the vertebral region confirm her stories of spinal surgery, stories I disdained and hardly believed when I came of age, growing into my own body and declaring independence from hers. These scars are proof of her physical pain, a condition that I, as a young adult, dismissed as one of my mother's many lies.

I never saw these scars because I never really looked at my mother's back, which was, unlike the front of her body, a wretched territory. Anyone would have turned away from it. First was the unsightly birthmark—a large triangle of hair—on her sacrum. Which one might have found charming had it not been for the cratered scars in her buttocks, which she had caused by injecting drugs subcutaneously, but which she said were caused by being ill and having to stay in bed for a long time. I believed this story until my father told me about her heroin addiction. I knew she was ashamed of her body because the birthmark and her buttocks were ugly, and she was obsessed with beauty. By turning away from her back, I thought I was being respectful. She may have interpreted this differently, may have thought she repulsed me, but worse is true: I pitied her for having such a thing that marked her and later, when I grasped what she had inflicted on herself, I loathed her for the violence required of such harm.

When I finished reading the part of the autopsy report confirming the first surgery, but not the subsequent five operations Dolores claimed to have had in conjunction with spina bifida, suddenly I wanted to know what really happened to her, so I spent days online, researching surgical procedures used to treat spina bifida in the 1930s and 1940s, only to come up empty handed. Besides, I finally concluded, what difference did it make if my mother had one or five operations? What did it matter if she had been born with a congenital defect such as spina bifida or if someone or something else—the driver of a vehicle, a relation or an acquaintance, a fall down a flight of stairs—had injured her? Even if she could no longer tell or, perhaps, even *know* the truth, the pain was real to her, and it was coupled with deep emotional turmoil. Like many people in extremis, she self-medicated. Certainly, she was not the first or last in my family to have followed such a path. The autopsy report describes multiple oval, depressed subcutaneous injection sites on her thighs and buttocks, evidence of the injectable opiate drugs she used to deal with that pain, and which she denied or admitted using depending on circumstances, her mood, the audience.

Errors in the report alarmed me: Dr. Charlot had recorded my mother's height as five feet and her eyes as light brown; in fact, she was five-nine with eyes that were almost black. What if, I wondered, the woman whose autopsy report I was reading was *not* my mother? Maybe Dr. Charlot was tired or incompetent, her observations thus flawed. Perhaps, I thought, I've believed all this time that my mother committed suicide when she didn't. This sense of collusion in a wrongdoing, I realize now, is not dissimilar to what I felt when I first learned that my mother died. Residual guilt— which I resisted like a person about to have an accident resists the idea of oncoming fatality—was causing my discomfort. The errors on these pages, I told myself, are simply errors. People are prone to blunder.

And anyway, the report provided answers I needed. The alteration of my mother's face—distorted to such a degree that I hesitated in confirming her identity—was caused by rigor mortis relaxing in the cold body and livor mortis settling into the right side of her face. The scars on her body testified to a life of pain, the dissatisfaction she felt with her physical self, and her belief that cosmetic surgery slowed aging. The cause of her death, suicide, was precipitated by an overdose of digoxin.

Questions emerged (and remain): Was the expression of terror—her mouth, stretched wide in the shape of an O, an image I cannot shake—caused by the "abnormal dreams or nightmares" reported by patients who have survived digoxin toxicity? Had she experienced the visual effects of digitalis overdose—hazy vision, yellow-green halos around objects— the kind of altered perception of color that some doctors believe affected Vincent Van Gogh? Prior to dying, were the objects she saw tilted at odd angles and bathed in waves of acidic color, like the painter's *Room at Arles?*

IX. *"the verbs surround me / like faces of strangers"*

After Dolores died, there was no time to step back and feel anything, and even if there had been, I'm not sure I would have known how. As it turns out, I have a delayed reaction to loss, my grief unfolding in geological time. The events surrounding my mother's death became a series of excruciating details to mind. She had broken many laws but she had died, and I had little time to figure out how best to protect myself. I was frightened of being sucked down the rabbit hole my mother had descended, and too many lawyers were saying too many things to me: my mother's attorney urged me to continue the insurance claim; my friend Roberta, a lawyer, advised me to be silent while her husband, also a lawyer, catalogued the contents of the apartment; my family friend Bob, the attorney who advised me to stop seeing or talking to my mother, asked to see the will; and counsel to the estate's representative handed me papers to sign.

Dolores had appointed as executor a woman named Betty, who became on March 29, 1989, the owner, with me, of the apartment on West Seventieth Street. Tapes playing in my head, of my mother's repeated stories about Betty's alleged ties to organized crime, made me wonder how much Betty knew about the insurance claim or the Medicare fraud, though I suspected she knew quite a bit. It occurred to me that this woman—named as co-owner of the apartment only a week prior to my mother's death—might have tried to blackmail Dolores. I decided to play dumb, a tactic learned growing up in the shadow of a woman whom I was unable to confront not only when she was alive, but, I was going to learn, for many long years after she died.

Even though I was innocent of any wrongdoing, my mother made me feel, because I was her daughter, guilty by association. In the panicky haze of the forty-eight hours following the identification of her body, I sorted through all her papers, in a fervent attempt to locate and then remove anything that might have made me appear guilty of being party to her fraudulent activities. A lot of stuff accumulates in a six-room apartment over the course of twenty years. And Dolores saved everything. In one closet, I found a large plastic bag filled with hundreds of Valium tablets. Boxes of shoes occupied the entirety of the king-size space beneath the bed. From another closet, I pulled off the shelf a carton filled with gifts I had made for her over the years—ceramic animals, pencil holders, handmade books—and the cards I had sent from places I lived that she had not visited.

These things constitute some of the fragments of Dolores: perpetual drug user and fashion-crazed mother. Two shows for the price of one. The filing cabinets contained the more revelatory documents. I discovered that my mother's claim to a fabricated identity was more complicated than I had imagined: She possessed three passports, each issued to a differently named woman and containing pictures of three differently hair-styled and made-up versions of Dolores (though her I-just-got-away-with-something smile is identical in all of them). I opened an envelope containing eight social-security cards, printed with the names of some of the women who had lived in the back bedroom of my mother's apartment, vulnerable young women whom Dolores had convinced to participate in her schemes, others belonging to aliases. On one of those cards was a version of my name.

All these facets of my mother's self refracted on paper exhausted me, my fatigue compounded by having to act like a stupid kid for Betty, who had proclaimed when she arrived, in spite of the nineteen-page letter and the shorter note I proffered, "This is *not* a suicide. I *know* suicide. My mother killed herself and it looked *nothing* like this."

Did she, I wonder now, really believe in a one-size-fits-all template for maternal suicide? Or was she, as I suspected then and still believe, trying to prevent me from contesting her inheritance of half the apartment? I'll never know for sure.

Dolores's friends—the same ones who had left messages on my answering machine—suddenly became unavailable when it came to such practical matters as helping prepare or set out the food they expected to eat after the service. But they made themselves heard when they learned that I had arranged for the memorial to be held at a Catholic church.

"Your mother was Jewish," one informed me in a tone that dismissed me as having any relation to my mother and at the same time indicted me for abandoning her. In terms of Jewish halakhic law, because my grandmother was Catholic, my mother was actually not Jewish, though she ignored this, purposefully claiming Jewishness when she circulated in certain circles of friends and acquaintances.

"Why would you do this?" another said. "So insulting."

Practically none of them had visited Dolores in recent months. Not one of them offered to help just after her death. My anger at these so-called friends was tempered by the humble silence of my Jewish cousins, who made their way from New Jersey and filed into the church silently, coats draped over their arms, the men in suits and ties; the women coiffed at their local beauty parlors and wearing those simple black dresses that hung in the back corners of their closets, wrapped in dry cleaner's plastic, waiting for occasions such as these.

Cora Townsend visited the day before the service. She had cleaned and shopped for Dolores before my birth and cared for me when I was an infant. She and my mother remained in touch over the years. My mother had told me several times about how Cora once saved my life. I had ingested some of the foam-rubber mattress stuffing in my crib and was choking. Cora just happened to come in and check on me.

"She held you upside down with one hand and reached into your mouth with one finger and pulled out the foam," my mother said. "Saving your life." After an appropriately long pause, she spoke again. "You were so tiny. You fit in the palm of her hand."

I never asked how my mother knew about this event. Was she there in the room, rendered helpless by a drug-induced stupor? Or was she coming down the hall and happened upon the scene? Did she dream it? Had Cora told her—and if she did, how did *she* tell this story?

Cora was a large black woman with large hands, though I realized as she stood in the foyer of my mother's apartment that her hands were only half as big as Dolores always described them. When Cora hugged me, she wrapped me in a scent of powder and lavender sachets, which gave me great relief and anguish. Relief because I knew her to have protected me. Anguish because we wouldn't have known one another had she not been a black woman needing a job, and my mother hadn't been a single, working white woman who needed help. Relief because the painful reality of those circumstances were suspended momentarily in our embrace. Anguish because our intersection was another episodic sojourn in the temporary geographies I've inhabited, and even though I wouldn't have admitted it then, I knew we'd never see one another again after this visit. Cora's memories of my mother spanned more than three decades. She was the only woman alive who knew me as a baby and then a toddler. We sat in my mother's kitchen and drank coffee. Her pocketbook, a massive, shiny leather thing that was more like a small chest, dominated the small table.

"I don't know how white folks do things when someone dies," Cora said, "but where I come from, food and all that comes from the neighbors. You shouldn't have to lift a finger, Kimmie."

I nodded, though Cora's bluntly offered knowledge about the slippery ways white folks did things surpassed mine, and we both sensed that nothing would happen the way she said.

In fact, just several hours before Cora's arrival, one of my mother's neighbors appeared at the door.

"I'm so sorry for your loss," the woman said, like an afterthought. "Anyway, I work at the Metropolitan Opera. Your mother had such beautiful hats and costume jewelry, and I was wondering if you might want to donate them to the opera."

I wanted to reach across the threshold and slap this stranger, and the thought crossed my mind that I could, with some degree of legality, slam the door on the woman's face and break her nose.

But my real emotional response was locked in another strata of my consciousness. I politely declined her request and closed the door.

Cora set her coffee cup in the saucer. I brought out all my mother's hats and offered them to her.

"This one," she said, holding up a bright pink straw lampshade hat decorated with an orange chiffon flower, "will be perfect for church in the summer." I nodded as she set the hat on her head.

"Do you know, Kimmie, I once took you with me to church?"

As she started speaking, I thought Cora might tell me a story about my mother being unable to leave her bed, or one in which Dolores disappeared overnight.

"When you was little, you walked up on your toes," she said. "What we call *ballet toes*. A bad sign…. So I took you to my congregation to be healed."

"What happened?" I asked.

Cora adjusted the hat, pulling it to an angle. Her gesture invoked all the begloved and hatted ladies of Harlem Sundays and stirred the residue of a memory that included the ferocious sanctuary of unconditionality.

"There was a mess of people that Sunday singing and testifying. I held you up—you was so tiny—and Reverend James, he blessed you."

"And?"

"You never walked like that again."

My mother hadn't told me this story. Perhaps Dolores *had* disappeared on that particular Sunday. Or maybe she was passed out cold from too many painkillers.

"You were healed," Cora said. She set the coffee cup in its saucer and looked at me. I want to believe she saw a young woman, scared and already tired, who had once been a baby and needed her surrogate love, but in her eyes I saw instead a recognition of how deeply memory had failed not only me, but her, us.

The tale about my "ballet toes" suggests that even as a toddler, I tried to appear bigger, or older, than I was, walking on my tiptoes in an attempt to be closer to adult size. After all, when we are that young, age expressed as time is a concept too abstract to grasp; instead we measure how old we are in terms of the concrete, our height. Cora knew children should be children, rooted in the ground, solid on two feet before reaching upward.

But Cora's telling of the story also safeguarded me in those first days after my mother's death, when I most needed emotional shelter. I wonder now what remains of that healing, if, somehow, such a curative experience can defend you in the future, and whether Cora knew then that I was going to need a shield—constructed of faith, or love, or simply the benevolence of a congregation of strangers—to take with me as I traveled through childhood and then past it into my late twenties.

DAY 2:
To Create Such a Ruin

Since we are dealing with humans and not
angels, we must take human frailties into account.
Granted that the mother is not perfect, still,
imperfection is not unfitness. And if we rejected
anything short of flawlessness, our quest would
have to go beyond and higher than this earth.

— *People ex rel. Geismar v. Geismar, 54.*
.Y.S.2d, 747, 756 (Sup. Ct. 1945)

Everyone knows along what edge I am,
like a sleepwalker, treading.

—*Anna Akhmatova trans. by Judith Hemshemeyer*
[March 19, 1969]

I. *"hearts charred as any match."*

"You'll understand our divorce when you're older," my mother was fond of saying, though she couldn't have predicted that her separation from my father would lead to her undoing.

I relate my parent's divorce to two of my only memories from early childhood, both set in the beginning of the 1960s. The first involves the days following John F. Kennedy's assassination, when footage of the funeral procession—the shiny black car wending its way through a crowd shocked into stillness—replaced the cartoons that normally aired on morning television. Had Bugs Bunny, that immortal trickster, died? It was the first time I saw an adult cry, and it seems fitting that I remember it was raining, even if it may not have rained, because it was my mother crying, and I probably believed then that tears and rain were related. My mother's wet face, bathed in the vaguely blue light of the television, is the representative image I always conjured in connection with the dissolution of our family.

The problem with this memory is that my parents divorced a year before JFK was killed, though for years I thought these events had occurred simultaneously. The divorce decree is dated November 1962, and Kennedy was alive and had made, thirteen days after the judgment was issued, a brief televised address informing Americans that the Cuban Missile Crisis had ended. This fact always startles me because I don't recall my mother or father ever discussing the political tensions of those days in October of 1962, though they both mentioned recollections of other historical events—the Depression, World War II, the Korean War—which occurred before I was born. I've often wondered how my parents reacted to the news. Neither of them ever talked about sitting on the edge of their seats as they followed the escalating potential of a nuclear showdown. Did the uncertainty and angst of being on a nuclear brink, which loomed during the last month of my parent's marriage, exacerbate all the dislikes they had cultivated for one another? And what if they had attempted reconciliation? Might they have resumed their roles in the little drama of married life in 1960s Manhattan as the news of the Cuban Missile Crisis unfolded over the radio and on television?

And what would such a scene resemble? It's morning. My father is positioned behind a newspaper at the kitchen table. On the Formica counter, a stainless-steel toaster distorts everything reflected on its rounded surface, including my mother's face, which is weighted with the kind of boredom that will lead to despair. No one, especially my father, can see any of that under the elaborate mask she has designed. She turns up the radio's volume. They are two separate human beings in the same apartment, the same city, the same country. Both of them probably hating the recognizable trope of a married couple they have become—a husband hidden behind the daily news, a wife surrounded by shiny appliances. Completely unable to face how they've become sequestered in a failed nuclear family in the atomic age, unable to retrieve their generation's take on the idioms about home (*a man's home is his castle; a woman's place is in the home; there's no place like home*). Each wondering for an instant if they'd made a mistake voting for Kennedy, both of them incapable of sharing even their small doubts about common political leanings. In this invented film of my parents, the tenor of their exchange resides in small talk.

"Pass the butter," my father says. His thick, Brylcreemed hair is visible above the newspaper's edge.

"There's a sale at Bonwit's today," Dolores says. Perhaps on her way home from work, she'll stop in. She pictures fingering a new blouse or scarf that will be neatly folded, wrapped in pale lilac tissue paper, and placed by the sales clerk into one of those now defunct white bags decorated with blue and purple violets. She notices the broadness of her husband's forehead, and for a minute, perhaps, remembers how his pale green eyes, a tender color in a face seemingly carved of stone, once startled her.

"I'll be late coming home, have a meeting." He glances at her. Dolores stands and pours coffee, wearing a dress that accentuates her narrow waist, all trace of the pregnancy vanished. Her blonde hair is swept up—he doesn't know what the style is called, but most of the women he knows wear their hair this way now—and she's already applied her makeup, her lipstick a coral color that reminds him vaguely of the Virgin Islands where they honeymooned and, as Dolores will tell it later, where they conceived their daughter. For a minute, he recalls the palm trees, that his wife wore dark sunglasses and a white button-down blouse over her swimsuit, and that he took picture after picture of her, knowing, even then, that she would never again be that beautiful. He had met her just after divorcing Ethel, who gave him two sons, to whom he now pays alimony (which he will pay until he dies, grumbling each time he signs those checks), who also wears her hair in the same fashion. And then he lowers his eyes back to the *Times*. He never considers that he ever *really* loved either woman, the two mothers of his three children, because if he did, he would have to admit that something has failed.

JFK's assassination occupied the front seat in my memory of that time, and while this astonished me once, it does not anymore. What we deem our first memory is more often the product of collective storytelling. For the most part, family members or caregivers construct our first recollections.

I discovered my real first memory while dusting. I was holding a can of Pledge, the brand name in sharp contrast with what I'd later determine as the subject of this memory, my parents' divorce. The odor of lemon furniture polish triggered a clear image of an oversized volume about dinosaurs, one of those Time-Life coffee-table books with paintings inside that unfold to reveal a panorama, in this case, the dinosaurs' march across time to extinction. I was two years old, perhaps, when I wandered alone into the living room, sat in front of the low coffee table, which had been dusted just hours earlier, and looked at that book. I touched the image of the dinosaurs walking into their own obscurity as if I might feel the scorch of the sun on their prehistoric hides.

As I reassembled the pieces of this recollection (the oily odor of lemon polish, the dark wood of the table, the seemingly resigned expressions of the dinosaurs under a white sun), I saw myself repeatedly returning to the living room to peruse that book, using repetition to secure a future emotional memory of my early childhood. I connected the extinction of the dinosaurs with the expiration of our little family. But there is more, I think: To expire is to breathe out, but it has come to mean the end. Extinction is both a process and an outcome. When I say *extinguish*, I often think of fire, because the origin of the word is "to quench," which I associate with thirst, liquid, the water used to put out a blaze. Air, fire, water. In this elemental view of my family, earth—what should have grounded us all—is missing.

I'm no longer surprised that memories merge together and collapse time. Eventually these recollections coalesced into an apt description of my childhood, an environment shaped by extinction in which no one explained the real reasons for anything. A place where memory was shaped like an oversized book or the curve of an Apatosaurus neck, all black and white and gray like a televised funeral cortege casting the palest indigo light onto my mother's wet face. All of it empty and pallid as a wasteland.

II. *"Your body / Hurts me as the world hurts God."*

On March 5, 1968, my father's attorney filed in the New York Supreme Court a writ of habeas corpus and petition on my behalf. I was eight years old. The petition addresses my mother and demands that she appear in court.

Habeas is the subjunctive form of the Latin verb *habere*, "to have." The subjunctive is not really a verbal tense, but a mood, and it suggests that the opposite of what is being declared is, in the mind of the speaker, also possible. Therefore, "you must have" is a statement that assumes the speaker is aware, or might suspect, that "you may *not* have." Such a writ sounds very dramatic: "We *command* you," the first line reads, "that you have the body of Kim Dana Kupperman, by you *imprisoned* and *detained*." As hyperbolic as it sounds, as a legal instrument, habeas corpus is one of the oldest and most common remedies used to challenge the terms of child custody or visitation.

It was a good strategy. Because a writ of habeas corpus must be filed in a state's Supreme Court (as opposed to civil court, where most family matters are adjudicated), my father's attorney was able to bypass the growing pains of the then-young family court system, and avoid a legal arena where my father had no connections, and thus no favors to cash in.

Indeed, my mother had the body—mine, that is. And though *imprisoned* is not quite the word that captures how she treated me, she certainly detained me from seeing my father on a regular basis, and her "illness" (as she referred to the drug addiction that kept her bedridden) resulted in a fair amount of neglect. In my mother's apartment, the curtains were always drawn, windows closed, most lights off. Sometimes she was too "ill" to get out of bed to feed me.

I couldn't have been much older than four when I climbed up onto the kitchen counter to eat dry, wheel-shaped noodles from the box. I can still see my hand reaching for the blue box with yellow letters and a cellophane window. *Ronzoni* was a word I could not yet read, but was familiar to my young eyes. I had eaten those wagon-wheel noodles after they were cooked soft in boiling water, so I must have deduced that it wouldn't matter if I ate them right out of the box. I had to hold one in my mouth until it softened enough to chew. They tasted a little like paste.

On those days when Dolores emerged from her bedroom to pretend that everything was okay and play at being a mother, she combed the tangles out of my hair. A photograph of one of those grooming sessions, perhaps taken by my mother's boyfriend at the time, shows us in the bathroom. Neither of us appears happy, which makes me wonder why Dolores kept the picture. I face the camera, hands clasped against my chest, my head tilted to one side, my expression one that beseeches the photographer to *please end this* before tears or tantrums occur. My mother is dressed in an uncharacteristic-for-her-taste *schmata*, a black bag of a house dress with white trim on the neck and arms, a garment that emphasizes her wan face and badly bleached long hair—she was at the height of her "illness" at this time—and hides the shapeliness and fashion that otherwise defined her. She concentrates on what must have been an impossible tangle at the back of my head (like Alexander the Great, who cut apart an insoluble puzzle with his sword, my mother once cut off all my hair after she could not pull a comb through it). Looking at this image, I can almost conjure a memory—of impatience on my part, frustration at my ingratitude on hers—to accompany it.

But, I wonder now, when my mother opened the envelope containing the writ of habeas corpus, did she find such language absurd when referring to a mother and child? *Of course I have my daughter's body*, she might have thought. *I produced this body.*

My mother told me the story of my conception when I was about thirteen or fourteen, long after the custody fights had ended and I no longer lived with her. This was the period of my adolescence before I learned she had been lying about anything and everything, before I realized that all she wanted to do was manipulate me to think or feel a certain way, before I distanced myself from her. She dropped then all pretense of mothering and tried instead to be my best friend. I don't remember doing homework on the weekends we spent together, though possibly the rule was to finish it Friday afternoon and review it for completeness upon my return home Sunday evening. The absence of responsibility meant doing as I wished, and my mother allowed me to hang out with my boyfriend in my bedroom with the door closed, smoke cigarettes and pot in the apartment, stay up late, things I was not allowed to do while in the care of my father and stepmother, Phoebe. Dolores and I confided in each other, which mostly meant talking about sex, though the only story of her sexual exploits that she told was the one about my conception.

"Your father and I were in the Virgin Islands on our honeymoon," she started. I always loved that irony: my parents in a place whose name suggests anything but—or, some might argue, everything related to—the celebration of marriage and the conception of a child.

"We were in bed, fooling around..."

I knew she was crossing a boundary by revealing something so private.

"'Say *fuck me*,' your father ordered. Well, Kimmie, of course I refused..."

Which I'm sure she did since my mother never used swear words.

"...and then he said it again, a little more harshly. His face looked mean. 'Say *fuck me*, Dolores,' but still I didn't say it. Your father then slapped me..."

She lowered her voice a notch, and paused to light a cigarette, to let her story settle in. I felt both attracted and repulsed to what she was telling me, a rubbernecker at the intentional accident of my own beginning.

"...he slapped me on the face. 'Say *fuck me*,' he yelled. His face was really mean. I said it...and you were conceived."

Such a story illustrates the complexity of my parents' relationship. And then there's the obvious dilemma of the story itself. It is entirely possible that my father did what my mother said he did. It's also possible that he didn't do any of it, as possible as him having done one of the two things, asking my mother to swear being the more benign action. Maybe some version of this scene actually occurred and was then embroidered, such narrative embellishment a quick fix in my mother's repertoire of different lies. But no matter what, that particular scene belongs to the private life of my parents. It is the kind of story which, after hearing, one might ask (or think), "What kind of mother tells her teenage daughter such a story?" And while this particular narrative didn't inflict on me any intense emotional harm, my mother knew that I would never forget it.

What I didn't—couldn't—realize when my mother told that story was how it would preface the hundreds of pages of court documents I saw three decades later, which my father gave me after I asked for them, relentlessly, each time I saw him. Papers he refused to extract from his locked filing cabinet until shortly before he died. My father kept this Secret File for over forty years. He moved it from New York to Massachusetts, then Connecticut, back to New York, and finally, to Florida. The bulk of the file consists of transcripts from a thirteen-month trial—initiated with the writ of habeas corpus in 1968—in which my father sued my mother for custody of me. Separation agreements, a Mexican divorce decree, affidavits and court orders, and several pieces of correspondence between my father and attorneys comprise the remainder. Pieces are missing—transcripts from a seven-day habeas corpus trial in 1965; items entered as exhibits; receipts for what was disbursed to pay for these legal proceedings.

III. "what a real man's heart is like"

The file contains a report authored in 1962 by a team of private investigators. This report reads like a B-movie script of a marriage gone awry. July 28, 1962: three men known as J. M., A. B., and C. L. observe my mother as she arrives in a hired black Cadillac at an attorney's office on Madison Avenue. They follow her when she leaves the building with my father and goes home with him to 300 Central Park West. A half hour later, they watch my father put my mother into a taxi, which she takes to Penn Station. After purchasing her ticket for the Bay Shore train, she buys a candy bar and waits on the platform. One of the investigators follows her onto the train. The other two drive with my father to Bay Shore, where they board the 7:00 pm ferry to Ocean Beach, Fire Island.

By car, the trip to Bay Shore takes about an hour; the ferry ride to Ocean Beach is another thirty minutes. At first I picture them dressed in suits, but then I figure they probably opted for more casual, less obvious apparel—sport jackets, slacks, no ties. My father was forty-eight; the others I place in their late thirties, not from any evidence in the report, but because it feels right to imagine my father as an older man who'd supervise the younger men paid to assist him in catching his wife—also younger, fifteen years his junior—at a game he regularly (but discretely) played.

They all smoke, though for my father, smoking meant a long Havana cigar, whose paper rings I coveted as a little girl. They travel in relative silence on this trip—I can't see my father saying much to these strangers about his life, though I'm sure he wondered whether any of the findings would make their way into public light and chip at his successful career as a fundraiser for Jewish philanthropies. The four men are together for a specific purpose, to catch my mother in an act of infidelity. In such a situation, there isn't a lot to say. Instead, my father probably makes a clicking noise in the back of his throat while jingling the change in his pocket. The air smells of salt and grass warmed by the sun. The man driving takes off his jacket and rolls up his shirt sleeves. The three of them buy tickets for the ferry, make their crossing without event, and settle in to watch "the subject," Dolores Kupperman.

At about 8:30 that evening, my mother emerges from her residence, wearing long white pants, a multicolored blouse, and a kerchief over her hair. She stops at a dress shop and then proceeds to a cottage known as the Doll House. Several minutes later, she leaves that residence with a male companion, one Manny Wolf, who holds her around the waist. Another couple emerges from the Doll House, and all four go to an establishment called Goldie's, where they sit at the bar until they are seated for dinner. At that point, the three investigators decide it would be prudent to avoid any potential recognition. They ask my father to leave the island.

"We'll go back to Bay Shore, Mr. Kupperman," says investigator A. B. "I'll go with you. We can take a water taxi."

By now, Abner Kupperman is furiously clicking the back of his throat, maybe even coughing.

After dinner, the investigators observe the two couples "skipping back to the Doll House," where they stay for ten minutes before returning to Goldie's. Another ten minutes pass, and Dolores rushes outside, crying. She runs to her bungalow and then rejoins the other couple at Goldie's, where she sits on the lap of her blonde friend's boyfriend and joins the group, laughing and singing. At this point, investigator C. L. telephones investigator A. B.

Keep in mind there were no cell phones in those days, so investigator A. B. was probably standing by a pay phone when C. L. called.

"It's heating up here," C. L. says to A. B. "Come back to Ocean Beach."

A half hour later, my mother leaves Goldie's and returns to the Doll House, where her male companion has remained. Then my father and investigator A. B. show up. The four men proceed to the rear of the cottage, enter through the unlocked back door, and approach the bedroom, where they are certain to find Dolores and her consort. My father opens this door while investigator C. L. takes a "photoflash picture of the female subject," who, he'll write later, "was against the wall side of the bed and the male subject, who was on the edge of the bed near the door." Then the four men dash out of the cottage and take a water taxi (conveniently waiting at the pier) back to Bay Shore, where they get into the car they left there, and drive back to New York.

The report is typed, single-spaced, on two pages of bond paper. No letterhead identifies this document as having been issued by a bona fide investigation team, nor do any signatures reveal the full names of A. B., C. L., and J. M. I find it curious that my father should have participated in the investigation. It occurs to me that he may have been alone, followed my mother, taken a blurry photograph, and authored the report himself. Or maybe his best friend Mike, my godfather, was with him.

There are particulars in the report that would be whimsical if they didn't appear in material used to substantiate my mother's adultery. The purchase of the candy bar at Penn Station, for example. What *kind* of candy bar? Did she eat it on the train? I never once saw my mother purchase or consume a candy bar. Then there's the *Doll House*, Manny Wolf, *Goldie's*, which is too absurd for me to absorb at first. At any moment, I expect Ibsen's Nora to appear, dressed in a red cape and hat, with blond hair. Looking just like my mother.

"You can't make this stuff up," a friend says to me after I call her and narrate this part of the Secret File. Never mind making it up, I have no idea what to *make* of it.

Other details provoke questions. The Madison Avenue address that appears in the beginning of the report is the same as that of my mother's attorney at the time. Were my parents discussing the terms of their soon-to-occur separation in that office? If that's the kind of meeting they were in, the tension between them in the taxi home must have been unbearable. Assuming that my father really had hired three private investigators, I wonder how he acted, how he spoke to my mother as he helped her into the taxi that took her to Penn Station.

"Have a nice evening, Dolores," he might have said flatly, thinking, *see you later*.

Why was my mother crying after spending ten minutes in the bungalow with her supposed paramour? Maybe Manny Wolf told her he was only in it for the sex. Perhaps he told her he wasn't interested in her anymore. What did the other blonde think when my mother sat on *her* companion's lap? *Get off, go back to your own man in the cottage?*

No amount of research will unearth the thoughts of the characters in this moody spectacle. The only behavior that resonates as belonging to my mother is that when she wasn't in bed with the curtains drawn and the lights off, she was always going out to "carry on," as my father called it, while someone else took care of me. Otherwise, this Dolores is unrecognizable. I rarely saw her eat sweets, nor did I ever see her in the kind of playful, affectionate-with-a-man mood described by the authors of the report. She never drank, save the occasional Brandy Alexander at a restaurant. She was not the kind of woman who skipped; in fact, she was so superstitious that to this day, whenever I walk in a city, I hear her advice.

"Don't step on a crack, Kimmie," she always said. "Or you'll break your mother's back."

IV. "What should be done with her?"

The Secret File is mostly composed of voluminous transcripts from the 1968 custody case—785 pages generated on seven days between March and December of 1968, with 112 pages devoted to a contempt-of-court hearing that started in May of 1969 and ended a month later. Three New York Supreme Court justices took part in these proceedings. The judges are all now dead. What little I know of these three strangers—two men and one woman—I know from their obituaries, their comments recorded during the trials, and the decisions they made in my interest.

Thomas C. Chimera heard the part of the case that granted the writ of habeas corpus, ordered the Family Counseling Unit to evaluate the home environment, and moved the matter toward trial. Imagine having *chimera* as a last name. I wonder if the justice ever felt compelled to explain that the word for the fire-breathing, lion-headed, goat-bodied, serpent-tailed monster, which was supposedly the personification of snow or winter, originally meant *year-old she-goat*. Perhaps he kidded with his clerks—or maybe lawyers arguing cases before him joked—that his decisions were fanciful illusions.

Chimera was elected to the New York State Supreme Court in 1959, the year I was born. On March 20, 1968, the justice suspected he might not see the Kupperman custody case to its conclusion. "The matter is referred to the Family

Counseling Unit," he ordered, informing my parents that the issue would be decided after the social worker's report was received, either by trial or by stipulation. "Not necessarily by me because it all depends upon how long this is going to take," he added. My mother, who appeared without an attorney, was contentious. "I certainly understand English very well," she retorted when Judge Chimera asked her if she understood that she would need to cooperate with the Family Counseling Unit, as well as submit to evaluations by impartial doctors and psychiatrists. When my mother made an under-the-breath comment about my father not having a "pertinent reason" for keeping me longer than what she said he had agreed to, Justice Chimera bristled.

"Madam," he said, "if you are going to make a judgment for me, don't ask me to share my pay with you because I don't plan to do that. I am not making a judgment, and I am not going to let you make it either."

Unfortunately, court records do not inventory the clothing worn by plaintiffs and defendants. Maybe my mother used her cane, necessary, she claimed, because her legs buckled, but which had the dual benefit of keeping her stable while taking narcotic painkillers and providing evidence of disability for the city's social workers. Appearance meant everything to my mother. What disguise did she choose; which persona? In the role of Physically Disabled Single Mother, she might have worn little makeup, covered her hair with a kerchief, kept the colors subdued (a navy blue dress, tan overcoat, slightly scuffed flats), used a plain wooden cane. Had she chosen Former Salon Executive, her hair would have been styled at a beauty parlor, her lips carefully colored fire-engine red; this Dolores would wear a Coco Chanel suit, eschew the cane for pumps and a matching alligator pocketbook. Or maybe she wore pressed brown slacks, an ivory silk blouse, and a tweed blazer, secured her hair in a French twist, kept the makeup in subtle mauves, toted a leather briefcase, and used a brass-handled cane to portray Falsely Accused Former Cosmetics Industry Consultant whose severe pain ended her marriage and career and was now culminating in the termination of her parental rights.

My father was outfitted as he would have dressed for the office, in a dark gray or blue suit, a crisp white shirt with *AJK* monogrammed on the pocket, and a silk tie. My stepmother, Phoebe, most likely wore something simple but classy, a pleated wool skirt that fell below the knee, a not-too-tight cashmere sweater over her pronounced bosom, Italian shoes with low heels.

The judge wore a black robe.

V. "Sorrow behind, sorrow ahead"

Francis J. Bloustein presided over the hearings between October and December 1968, issuing the final judgment in April 1969 that granted custody to my father.

When the writ of habeas corpus was served to my mother in March of 1968, I was living with her. However, there had been a period of fourteen months in 1966-67 when she had handed me over to my father and Phoebe. According to my father, she said she was unable to manage me. In my mother's version of this episode, she informed my father that she needed medical treatment, hoping he would agree to look after me during her hospitalization. Regardless of who was telling the truth, after those fourteen months, my mother decided she wanted me back; she came to my school one afternoon in a taxi and took me home with her.

The trial started in October of 1968 but had already been on the docket five different times since March, rescheduled because my mother claimed to need a different lawyer. She knew this tactic would infuriate my father because he was paying an expensive attorney, and she probably hoped it would jeopardize Phoebe professionally since she had to take more and more time off from work to testify. On October 23, my mother tried to secure yet another adjournment, on the grounds that her attorney was not trying the case as she wished, and by that she meant he was not calling all the witnesses she wanted, believing that with their testimony she could not only outsmart my father, but make a good show for the court as well. She dismissed counsel, but Judge Bloustein requested the lawyer to remain by my mother's side—to protect her rights, he noted—as my father's attorney put in a prima facie case.

Dolores was not a woman who took *no* for an answer. She tried to argue with the judge, and though the transcripts lack description of her facial expressions, I can see her clearly. Angry that things weren't going her way, my mother suddenly appeared taller than she was; her already dark brown eyes went almost black. I had seen my mother morph into that larger-than-life rage, and it frightened me. If Isabella Neil, the victim of the hammer attack, had been in the courtroom just then, she might have said that her assailant had that same menacing countenance, that same molten look in her eyes.

"Look, madam," the judge said, "I am not going to take dictation from you." By virtue of sitting on a raised bench, Bloustein towered over not just my mother, but over everyone else in the room, mitigating the sense of threat that one party might have leveraged against the other. After asking that the Kupperman case be called, he addressed her again. "Sit down, Madam," he instructed. "Give her a pad. She can make notes," he said to the bailiff.

Francis Bloustein immersed himself in the sordid details of our lives over the course of five days at the end of autumn 1968. He listened to the testimonies of my father, Phoebe, and the parents of one of my childhood friends. He listened to my mother's witnesses, including a neighbor, her first cousin, her best friend (also my godmother), an ex-lover/business partner, a former childcare provider, and a doctor. And Judge Bloustein heard my mother's version of things as well.

The attorneys asked questions intended to substantiate or undermine the credibility of each of my parents. Custody cases are trials of character, really, and so my father accused my mother of being unfit, while my mother accused my father of lying. Phoebe was the only person who testified specifically about me, and in particular, she focused on the state of my physical and emotional being. She was a child psychologist and perhaps the most reliable witness in the courtroom.

Phoebe described a pitiful child.

"At age seven, she weighed forty-one pounds, exactly what she weighed at five and a half," she told the court. "She did not care to eat, or sit still, or sit and eat at the table. When she came to visit, her hair was frequently dirty and matted, underclothes torn and ragged. She picked at her body until it bled and scabs formed. She wet the bed every night, and was embarrassed. She was unwilling to bathe or brush her teeth. She didn't want to comb her hair. She didn't want to look in the mirror."

According to Phoebe's testimony, in first grade, I stopped up the toilets in school; the year these court proceedings started, I set a fire under the bed.

"When she came to live with us for fourteen months," Phoebe said, "Kimmie did not want to go to school. She stood in the doorway with her little hands on her little hips and said, 'I won't go.'"

At Christmas, she testified, I became agitated because of a card sent by a man who was the superintendent of my mother's building. I asked Phoebe if I really had to sit on his lap and kiss him. "He's always trying to kiss me," I told her. Though I do not recall the card and the requests for kisses, my memory of Jack Albrecht is clear. He wore cheap, navy blue polyester pants pulled up high over his waist. His face was sallow, white hair cropped close to his skull, eyes sunken, lips pale. He always wanted to take Polaroids of me, which made me uncomfortable when my mother left us alone and he took not one or even five, but twenty or thirty pictures in an hour.

Later, when I was in my twenties, my mother told me that before Jack Albrecht worked at the building where we lived, he had been convicted of molesting children. Dumbstruck, I never asked her why she ever left me alone with him. I knew by then that she was unable to answer such a question.

"It was impossible for anyone not to see that this child was deteriorating," Phoebe told the court.

"Strike out *deteriorating*," Judge Bloustein ordered. I like to think he said this against his own good judgment, that his voice was softer than usual. But the word is still on the page and maybe even was doubly on his mind once he called attention to it. I *was* deteriorating, failing to thrive. It exhausts me just to think about who I was then, a child retreating from life, who looked like she never slept or bathed or ate with any regularity. A daughter who was frantic and afraid, yearning for maternal supervision and guidance. While I recall one reaction only, wetting the bed, I do not remember being that little girl. One way that memory protects us, perhaps, is by disappearing.

Phoebe was the best witness my father could have had. She had saved notes I wrote to her, drawings I made, and a story I authored about a rabbit who had been chased by dogs and hunters but felt safe at home. These were all entered as evidence.

"In my opinion," she said, "this story expresses Kim's feelings." The justice did not strike from the record that subjective observation.

Phoebe also produced a list I had made. My mother objected, claiming it was not my handwriting, but when Phoebe testified that I had written the list on New Year's Eve, in the presence of my father, grandmother, and herself, the judge allowed it to be entered as an exhibit. In the list, I identified how I felt about my family. My mother was not mentioned.

"Did anyone ask her to do this?" my father's lawyer asked.

"No," Phoebe said, "she always sits and writes and draws."

When I was nineteen, Phoebe gave me a drawing I made at age six, an artifact that she did not submit to the court, but saved for when she thought I would be mature enough to make use of the information she planned to impart. On a piece of my father's note stationary—with *Memo from Abner J. Kupperman* printed at the top—I had drawn a girl with a forced smile and oversized hands in the middle of violent scribbles.

"She has no feet," Phoebe pointed out. "You must have felt trapped, that you could not escape the danger."

The miniature versions of who we become as adults are always available, if we pay attention. As soon as I could write, I made lists and stories. And before recognizing the power of words, I drew messages.

VI. *"everyone knew that the moment was at hand."*

Because my mother did not have an attorney for the first day of the custody hearing, my father, Phoebe, and two of their witnesses took the stand and testified without being cross-examined. Three weeks later, my mother brought a lawyer named Sidney Koblentz. I cast him as a lunchtime Scotch drinker (straight, no chaser), with a taste for beautiful women, fast cars, and expensive suits. He attempted to undermine Phoebe's credibility by using her professional credentials to undo her testimony.

"Mrs. Kupperman, in your occupation as a child psychologist, isn't it a fact that young children frequently object to bathing?" Koblentz asked.

"Yes."

"Isn't it a fact that it requires considerable urging for children to brush their teeth regularly?"

"Yes."

"What causes bed-wetting, or is it a natural thing with a child?"

"It can rarely be physical, but it sometimes is. Bed-wetting is a psychogenic symptom," Phoebe answered. My father's lawyer probably saw what was coming. Attorneys who spend many years arguing custody cases must have an ear for this sort of cross-examination.

"Well, it is not an unusual condition for children of the age of seven or seven and half years, am I correct?" Koblentz asked.

"I don't know the statistics on it, but I would say it was fairly unusual. Enuresis can come from a number of problems in children that age, but usually there is some psychogenic problem that accounts for it."

"It could come, of course, from separating a child from its mother, could it not?"

"There is a possibility that this could happen, yes."

Here my mother leans back a little in her chair, scoring a silent victory, appearing a little taller. Phoebe might have looked then at my father, an apology pulling down the corners of her eyes and mouth, an expression only he could translate. Koblentz was relentless. He went after the part of her testimony about my weight. I wonder if he knew that Phoebe struggled with her own weight, and if he did know, if it was because I might have told my mother that Phoebe was often on a diet.

"If two parents were of a slim or slight nature or stature, it would be conceivable that their child might also be of a similar nature?" Dolores's attorney asked.

"Yes."

Then he questioned Phoebe's intent to raise me "in the Jewish faith," and if, because she was no longer able to bear children, that was why she urged my father to seek custody of me. He even asked her if, in the context of her work with the Child Guidance Bureau of the City of New York, she knew the psychiatrist who evaluated my mother in connection with the hearing. There were no questions from

Mr. Koblentz about Christmas cards from strange men, the lists or stories or drawings I made. He based his entire cross-examination of Phoebe on innuendo. That struck-out word, *deteriorating*, must have lingered, even in a sleazy lawyer's mind, as an apt professional opinion, one surely confirmed by the social worker's report, a document alluded to during the hearing that only Judge Bloustein was permitted to read, and which I will never see because it was not included in any file, secret or otherwise.

VII. *"An accidental guest in this dreadful body."*

At my mother's behest, Koblentz called six witnesses. Two of them—Dolores's best friend (my godmother) and her ex-boyfriend—were caught in lies when cross-examined. The doctor who took the stand also did more harm than good, describing my mother as a woman whose opiate addiction was registered with city officials, and for a good number of years, and unlikely to dissipate. The physician probably felt lucky to not have his medical license revoked after my father's attorney uncovered one contradictory story after another.

Koblentz used a strategy informed by what Dolores related to him as the truth. Her drug addiction (the primary reason offered by my father's counsel for her unfit mothering), she maintained, was caused by legitimate pain from multiple operations necessitated by the congenital birth defect spina bifida. Her chronic pain, along with residual back problems, was the basis for her state-certified disability. When Koblentz put my mother on the stand, he started with questions about her medical conditions, questions she was able to answer with authoritative vocabulary and ease.

"Congenital spina bifida is an opening on the spine," she explained, very soon after being sworn in and taking the stand. "Mine was located on the first, second, third, fourth lumbar areas, which means from the waist to the coccyx.

That means at birth there were no vertebrae in the first, second, third, fourth vertebrae areas."

"Did there come a time that you underwent surgery as a result of this condition?" Koblentz asked. Though I can't tell how he sounded from the transcripts, I hear his voice when he questions Dolores as softer, his diction slower, than when he cross-examined Phoebe.

"Yes."

"And what procedure was used, if you know?"

"I know very well," Dolores said. "They took the tibia from my right leg and used that as a donor graft for my spine and I was told at that time that this was the first of a series of fusions to fuse the spine completely."

Almost 30 percent of my mother's testimony focused on *her* body. I read these pages, comparing what she said with the autopsy report, which describes major scars and thus confirms the first surgery, but not the subsequent five operations she testified to have had in conjunction with her spina bifida. Koblentz never asked her any questions concerning the condition of *my* body, an omission that suggests he suspected she would make a lousy witness because she was such an absent mother. The point of her testimony about hospitalizations and surgeries was to prove not only that she was intelligent but that she was lucid as to why she required opiates to alleviate chronic pain, and that my father—whose father, brother, and sister were doctors and who had been a pre-med student in college—was aware of her medical condition and simply did not care if she suffered or required intervention.

Bloustein listened to the entire case. He read the reports from the Family Counseling Unit. He interviewed my parents.

Of the three justices, he was the only one I met, when he summoned me to his chambers on my ninth birthday. I suppose he wanted answers, seeing, perhaps, that the adults in this case were overcome by their passions to the point of potential unreliability.

The day of that meeting, my mother woke me.

"Your birthday party is cancelled," she said.

"Why?"

"Your father has made arrangements for you to go to court today. He insists that you meet the judge. I'm sorry, sweetheart."

I believed her and she had me. Upset by this seemingly sudden turn of events, I was receptive to her instruction to tell Justice Bloustein how desperate I was to live with her; she even made me rehearse my answers. But I have no recollection of what I actually said to the judge. Matters discussed in chambers are off the record; the words uttered that day are buried with Francis Jerome Bloustein. Of that encounter I remember only climbing what seemed like endless steps in front of the courthouse at 60 Centre Street in lower Manhattan.

After inheriting the Secret File and examining the documents, I discovered that eighty-two pages were missing. The break in the narrative came at page 504, recorded on December 18, 1968. Which is why I climbed, forty years later, those same steps at 60 Centre Street and went to the basement and into the records room. I didn't know it at the time, but I was about to retrieve a memory, though it was recorded by someone else.

The eighty-two missing pages included briefs filed by the lawyers and letters written by my mother to the judges, pleading with them to reinstate me into her care. But the real "find" was the fifteen-page judgment authored by Justice Francis Bloustein, in which he briefly describes his interviews with me, which occurred in the absence of counsel: "On both occasions," he wrote, "the child indicated that she was ambivalent about who she wanted as her custodian."

Ambivalent. I've used this word before to describe the relationship with my mother. It is a word that suggests, of course, an absence of power. Which is what happens when memory redacts scenes and conversations but retains a feeling of ambiguity so pronounced that it might be noticed by a stranger.

VIII. *"The quality of mercy is not strained"*

Justice Margaret M. Mangan presided over the four appearances in the spring and summer of 1969, when Dolores was charged with contempt of court after failing to return me to my father after her weekend visitations. In 1932, Margaret Mangan was one of the first women admitted to the New York Bar Association. In 1967, she made headlines when she ruled that a husband could not receive alimony from his ex-wife. "A husband who looks to his wife for support is placed in an unnatural relationship," she wrote, though she herself had never married.

My mother might have thought some bargain could be struck—here was a single woman, a Catholic too, sitting on the bench; and there was my mother, a single mother, half Catholic, pleading for the return of her only child. But it didn't work out that way. Justice Mangan, whose penchant for children's safety was underscored when she ruled that landlords, not tenants, were responsible for installing window guards in New York City apartments, was more interested in my welfare than forming allegiances with Dolores Kupperman, though after the third violation of the custody agreement, the judge still did not wish to punish my mother for contempt of court.

"Your little Kim is the ward of the court," she told my mother, "and I am in a superior *in loco parentis* role with respect to [her]." Though she had no children, the judge did not hesitate to give Dolores some parenting advice. "If parents only knew that children don't love; children *receive* love. That is the nature of children."

My mother must have burned inside hearing those words, issued by a woman who also said that "power speaks and does not have to explain." Perhaps that is why Dolores disobeyed Judge Mangan and orchestrated my fugue five days later.

I recall very well that Sunday evening in May: My mother informed me that I would not be returning home, but staying with her. She took the phone off the hook and instructed me to leave it that way. "Your father will come here tomorrow and ring the doorbell. You are not to answer it, you are not to make any noise."

Even then, way before I ever saw the kind of rage that transformed my mother's body and face, I knew not to disobey Dolores.

"If you want to live with me, you must do this. And you do want to live with me, Kimmie, don't you?"

I nodded yes, though I knew her plan was all wrong, that my father would somehow find out, and that she was making me do something untruthful that I did not want to do. I was afraid at that moment to say no. If I could have seen then what is now evident to me, that she had manipulated me to believe I wanted to live with her, I probably would have obeyed her anyway.

"When you see your father, you'll tell him you were dropped off in front of his building, but instead of going upstairs, you took the bus across town and went to Gabby's, where you hid in her bedroom."

That Sunday night, my mother and I rehearsed the story she had invented.

"Where were you Sunday night?" she asked

"At Gabby's. She hid me in her closet."

"Why didn't you go to your mother's?"

"She wasn't there, she went to New Jersey on Sunday."

"Usually your mother waits in the lobby until your father comes down to get you. Why didn't she wait there this time?"

"Her friend Vivian said she'd give me a ride. She let Vivian take me to my dad's."

"Say *father's* instead."

"Vivian took me to my father's. But when we arrived, there was no place to park so I got out and told her I'd be okay....Is that better, Mommy?"

"Why didn't you go upstairs when you were dropped off?"

"Because I want to live with my mother....right?"

"When you talk about me, say *Mommy*."

"Because I want to live with Mommy."

The next morning, my father came and repeatedly rang the bell, banged on the door, called my name. My mother watched him through the Judas hole until he left, and then she shuffled down the hall in her slippers and went back to bed. I spent the day in front of the television, and when my mother didn't get up to make supper, I quietly left her apartment, went to a neighbor's, and called my father. He arrived in ten minutes.

My mother's attempts to prove that I wanted to live with her only irritated Justice Mangan. "The Court doesn't make idle words," she said at the June hearing, where she found Dolores guilty of contempt, and punished her by ordering visitation in my father and Phoebe's apartment. Surely at that moment Margaret Mangan made eye contact with my mother. "The quality of mercy is strained," the judge continued, "so that I look upon this merely as a violation of a directive of a Court that was sympathetic to Mrs. Kupperman when the third visitation was violated, but the fourth violation, there is no excuse." *The quality of mercy is strained.* Certainly, my mother was shamed; she had stretched the judge's patience and burnt a bridge. Dolores would attempt some months afterward to mount an appeal, an endeavor she eventually relinquished when she realized I was thriving in my father and Phoebe's care and, more importantly, that I was liberated from her gravitational hold.

On page sixty-five of the 1969 transcripts, my father's attorney introduced a letter into evidence. My father explained that I wrote it as an apology for having lied about where I was when he was ringing the doorbell that Monday morning. When he picked me up that afternoon, I followed my mother's instructions and told him I had hidden in my friend's room, but my father could tell the story was untrue. He told me it was important to tell the truth, no matter the outcome. I do not remember the relief that surely ensued when I finally told him what happened. Nor do I recall the punishment he would later describe for the court: no television or phone calls for three days, which he said I tried to get out of by writing the apology. My father stood firm; there was no deal-making where a lie was concerned. I wrote the letter anyway, and I found this note preserved with the records in the basement of 60 Centre Street.

"Dear Daddy," I had written in a shaky, troubled script with no resemblance to my present-day controlled and calligraphic print, "I told you a lie and I'm sorry. I won't tell you anymore lies […] I am sorry I did not come to the door when you were ringing. But Mommy wouldn't let me. I love you both."

Almost ten years old, and already I had worked out that an act of writing might alleviate guilt, help me work out some interpersonal problem, make peace, if not with someone else, at least within myself.

There was a second letter discussed before Justice Mangan. My mother testified that I had sent a letter to the judge, explaining that my father had forced me to sign a letter stating I was in my mother's apartment from the Sunday to Monday in question. Of course, Margaret Mangan never received such a letter, and though my memory is incomplete, I am willing to swear that this particular missive was another of my mother's many fictions.

IX. *"this barren enterprise"*

Ultimately, the papers from my father's Secret File provide a clearer sense not of my memory, but of how frenetic my childhood was, and how my parents reacted to that chaos. Abner and Dolores were normal only in their complexity, and so entirely caught up in bitterness and anger that they could not see how strange it was that the determination of my upbringing had become a matter for strangers to arbitrate.

My mother didn't decide to perjure herself to keep me; she came to the hearing a chronic liar and was caught, though she never admitted that her lies had anything to do with losing custody of me or our eventual periods of estrangement. Her lying, I believe now, was not the product of malevolence, but a survival strategy used to cope with some trauma I will never confirm, no matter how many documents or files or dossiers I uncover. She believed the truth would harm her. And, there was the pathology of her drug addiction, for which lying is requisite.

My father wasn't a paragon of truth either, but he was well practiced at appearing virtuous, able to conceal his more unsavory behavior from public scrutiny (he was a compulsive gambler who happened to have business connections in or near Las Vegas), or to mask it in social convention (he married six women, disguising, he thought, his penchant for what his third wife—who outlived him—bluntly calls "womanizing").

Also, not to state the obvious, but my father was a man. He enjoyed the privileges accorded men, privileges that included looking the other way when he did things that most women would not get away with then.

When Dolores was no longer able to adequately care for me, she was forced to surrender my body to my father. Which is why one of my few memories about living with my mother is focused on the instant our being together ended, with an incident I call The Exchange, when Dolores took me to my pediatrician's office and handed me over to my father.

At Dolores's request, her father, Buxie, flew to New York to be there. He hated my father almost as much as he disliked his only daughter. He was to meet us at Dr. Stone's office.

That morning, as I dressed, my mother coached me. "As soon as your father tries to leave with you, start screaming that you want to live with me. Throw a tantrum."

"Okay, Mommy."

"If he picks you up, kick. Keep screaming." I nodded.

We took a taxi. I liked Dr. Stone. His bald head shone, he talked in a soft voice, and, after administering shots, he handed out lollipops. My mother and I arrived in time to spend several minutes alone with my grandfather, whom I seldom saw. When my father came through the door, my mother's father stood up, posturing.

"Sit down, Buxie," my father said to my grandfather. "Don't get in the way of this. It's not your business."

My grandfather puffed his chest, tugged at his jacket, and smoothed his hair with the heel of his hand.

"Good-bye, Kimmie," he said, looking down at me. "Here's some money, kid." He gave me a five-dollar bill, a fortune.

I was stunned. My mother glared at me.

"I don't want... to go..." I stammered. She kept glaring. "I don't want to go," I repeated, a little more vehemently. "I want to live with my mommy." My throat was dry. Then Dr. Stone came in, offering a lollipop. Cherry, my favorite.

My father reached for my hand. I held back.

"Come on sweetheart," he said. I searched his face for signs of anger, but all I saw was the handsome, familiar face I liked. Still, I shook my head no, clutching the lollipop in one hand, the five in the other. "We have to leave," he tried again.

"I don't want to go. I want to live with Mommy," I yelled, surprising Dr. Stone and myself.

Then my father picked me up. My mother gave me that molten-eyed look that my grandfather would tell me a decade later was how you identified a psychotic person. ("And you know what I'm talking about. You've seen it," he would say.)

I started my pretend tantrum, screaming that I didn't want to go, flailing my arms and legs all the way out of the office, in the elevator, and on the street.

"Settle down, sweetheart," my father implored. He set me down. I started crying, for real.

He hailed a taxi; I sobbed. Once we were inside the yellow cab, he gave me his handkerchief. I fingered the raised threads in the initials *AJK* monogrammed on the washed-soft fabric and watched the city streets pass by in the blur of tears.

DAY 3:
There is no mother there
And I have to give birth to her

We are only falsehood, duplicity, contradiction;
we both conceal and disguise ourselves from
ourselves.

—*Blaise Pascal*

Just don't give me a shameful ending
To my shameful life.
—*Anna Akhmatova trans. by Judith Hemshemeyer*
[Decade of the 1910s]

I. "And not to have is the beginning of desire."

April 7, 1958, 7:00 AM

Dolores sits in front of the mirror, contemplating the disguise she will wear today. First she must "put on her face," a quotidian practice at which she excels, though this routine seems to have more import on this day because she will leave the apartment in several hours, masquerading as another woman whose costume she has prepared these last four days, secreting away from her office the wig and the white beautician's uniform required for today's role.

"It's just theater," Dolores tells herself, something her father used to say when he was teaching her, his only child, how to work a room.

As she opens jars and sets out brushes on the vanity table, she fancies herself the perfect combination of stage actress and surgeon, daring on one hand, distant and exacting on the other. When Dolores looks in the mirror, instead of her reflection in the glass, the memoried images of other faces appear: one belongs to David, the man she should have married, the other to Isabella, his wife of six months, that redhead, the woman who is the focal point of today's performance. *If only you had stayed in New York with David,* Dolores thinks; *if only you hadn't insisted on going to Los Angeles for six months*—he wouldn't have met Isabella, wouldn't have fallen for her foreign charms. The redhead's face, Dolores admits, is lovely: porcelain complexioned; hair the color of new pennies (*new pennies*, she thinks, you can do better than that, but still, it's true); green eyes; prim nose. Dolores's hair is bleached, her eyes are dark; she paid to have her nose remade. She—well, not her really, but the person she is composing and building this morning in front of the mirror—*she* will hurt the redhead's face today. If *she* could tear it off, *she* probably would. Instead *she* will settle for scarring it, knowing that once Isabella's lovely face is bruised and damaged, David will remember how he said he couldn't live without the velvet dark of Dolores's eyes, that he would never love anyone else as he loves her, that she is the only one.

"Please, please, Dolores," he'll say, "I made a terrible mistake." He will even be grateful for the removal of the obstacle that separated them, though the child the redhead is carrying will be a problem. *If you're lucky*, Dolores thinks, *what happens later this morning will scare that baby out of Isabella, and David will be forever unlinked from her, free to be yours, again and as it should be.* She imagines how he will apologize and whisper how thankful he is for her forgiveness, how he will touch his lips to her neck, and the bad part of what will happen today will not matter because she will have won him back.

Dolores starts with foundation, dabbing it onto her cheeks, forehead, nose, and chin, as if her face were a compass, blending it over the skin with deft fingertips. "Preparing the canvas," she calls it, a technique she has taught so many women at Revlon's department-store makeup counter. Thank goodness those long days are over, she thinks, all that standing and smiling, pretending that those older women, the ones in their furs with too much time on their hands, really looked younger after she worked the "magic" of makeup on their wrinkled brows and sagging chins. All that smiling—a sure way to develop laugh lines and crow's feet. Dolores remembers how David helped her land the job, only four years ago. So much has happened between then and now, she's lost track. She was here in Manhattan and then she went back to L.A., or at least that's what she tells herself, and before she left, things were right; she was on the road to marrying him. And it all changed so quickly.

Dolores's eyes are almost black, like the trunks of trees darkened with rain. She wishes she had pale green eyes like the redhead, which is certainly how David was lured. What is it about light-colored eyes that so captivates?

On the nightstand sits this month's issue of *Good Housekeeping*, where David works. "For Personal Reasons" is advertised on the cover as a "Daring, Dramatic Novel. Complete in this Issue." It's really a short story, by Margaret Culkin Banning, but to sell the magazine, someone has stretched the truth. Probably David. He's good at that. "Regrets," Banning once wrote, "are as personal as fingerprints."

Which is why you must not forget to wear gloves today, Dolores tells herself. There must be no trace.

Once the foundation has set, Dolores applies the powder. She needs to replace the puff, an errand she might run later today, after she's completed what she needs to do. She smiles that picture-worthy, model-actress smile of hers and rouges the cheeks, not heavily, just enough to give an impression of having blushed. She read once that Darwin discovered blushing is a physical manifestation of shame, and today, Dolores doesn't want to look as if she's embarrassed; she doesn't want to stand out in that way. Rather she wants to blend in with the crowds of people who will be going to work when she leaves her apartment.

She lights a cigarette and places it in the ashtray. As it burns, she applies the tiniest dot of petroleum jelly to her eyelids, and then brushes on the eye shadow, her own special mixture of assorted beige and taupe face powders. She smokes the cigarette, contemplating for the nth time that if she had only stayed in Manhattan with David, none of this would be happening. Dolores considers blaming her father—he had asked her to come back to L.A. and help him with his latest scheme, and for personal reasons, the kind she can't divulge to anyone, she agreed. *And anyway,* she thinks, *you can't blame Buxie, he's your father.* Even if he's not that honest or the most respectable man, he did include her, and besides, she made some quick cash.

The fact is that you were blindsided, Dolores thinks. David had her convinced he only had eyes for her—he sang that song before she left and somehow even managed to procure one of those only-released-to-radio-station recordings by Peggy Lee, which he gave her.

"Here's a little gift, D," he said, all dapper and smelling handsome and clean.

Dolores played the record and he hummed along. "Are the stars out tonight? / I don't know if it's cloudy or bright"—what a silly song! She promises herself she will never be duped again.

She lines the eyelids: a fine stroke on the top lid, just to the corner. Dolores is an architect of disguise, a mask-maker extraordinaire. She takes a final pull on her cigarette before extinguishing it. She sweeps the mascara onto the lashes, the eyes beneath them so dark, their brown "unending," as David had once told her. *And you had believed him,* Dolores thinks, though she knows she had already learned about the dishonesty of men, starting with her father, her various love interests previous to David, then David himself, the one she believed wouldn't be like all the rest. *Fool.* Now the only way out is to hurt that pretty redhead. Dolores stands. In the kitchen, the coffee has finished percolating. She pours herself a cup. She takes it black, though it's really dark brown. She goes into the living room and puts that record on the turntable. "Are the stars out tonight," Peggy Lee sings, her voice as smooth and clean as milk, the piano's liquid notes and guitar's twang causing Dolores to ache for David's hand on her cheek, his gaze on her face. She knows she is making this up, but it's also real. She allows it to be true.

"My love is blind to everything, but you," Peggy sings. *Enough,* she thinks, *enough of this sentimental nonsense.* She removes the record from the turntable, throws it on the floor, and from her pocketbook, removes the hammer she placed in the bag last night, which she will use later this morning to complete the one prominent task on today's to-do list. She smashes that foolish record with the hammer. From the kitchen she gets the dustpan and she brushes up the shards of her disdainful rage. Into the trash those pieces go. *Good practice,* she thinks as she drops the hammer into her handbag.

Dolores returns to the bedroom. No need to style her hair today; a wig will conceal it. She uses a hair net to contain her only-my-hairdresser-knows-for-sure blonde waves. Very few people know that she is not a true blonde. She's even deceived David, the Prince of Pretend, with his fancy job at a ladies' magazine, how tricky of him. *You should have seen it coming,* she thinks.

The wig frames the face of a featureless, plastic head standing on the corner of Dolores's vanity table. A wig of black hair, cut in a bob. She will cover it with a green and white scarf, a gift from David. She imagines how the scene might play out if he had given his redheaded wife the same scarf. Dolores pictures the perplexed look on Isabella's pretty face when she only partially recognizes the scarf but can't place the woman wearing it, loving her confusion when the stranger (the *she* Dolores is creating this morning) appears at the door and asks to use the phone, yearning to see that puzzlement replaced by the recognition in Isabella's eyes that her husband has tricked her.

Dolores fits the wig onto her head and in an instant, she has become a different woman. She needs another name. Kate? No. Too plain, too girl-next-door nice. Ellen? Too close to Eleanor, her middle name. Laura? Too Otto Preminger. She squints her eyes and looks at the woman looking back at her from the mirror. She looks fierce. Black hair and dark brown eyes, alabaster skin. Carmen, she decides: a fiery gypsy; a woman who wreaks havoc. Dolores forgets just now, perhaps conveniently, that in the opera, it is Carmen who is murdered.

"Forgive her," she whispers, a slight shadow of a smile on her lips, "she knows exactly what she is going to do."

II. *"The fiction that results from feeling."*

April 7, 1958, late morning

"We'd gone around together back in L.A.," David Neil tells Detective Edward Brady of Manhattan's Eighteenth Precinct.

Brady learns later that Neil was involved with the suspect for four or five years (though he was never clear on *how* they met), that their time together was interrupted when Dolores Buxton returned to Los Angeles. During her absence, David met the German-born Isabella, a "slender redhead." Brady knows the Neil fellow was leaving out details, but the long and short of it was that he had wriggled free from the blonde and married the redhead. *Some guys are just unlucky*, Brady thinks.

The two men are sitting in Neil's office at *Good Housekeeping*, where the thirty-year-old Neil works as assistant promotion manager. Brady, unsure what Neil does exactly, guesses it relates to advertising. The guy seems slick enough for that kind of thing. He *was*, after all, hooked up with Dolores Buxton, the woman they are holding on charges of felonious assault. What a broad—a "shapely blonde," the *Daily News* will probably call her, Brady thinks, but love-crazed and dangerous—the kind of woman who is trouble, the kind of trouble men love getting into but loathe getting out of.

"Why would a guy work at a ladies' magazine?" Brady's partner, Jack Hanford, asked earlier.

"Why do you think?" Brady said. Hanford was a pretty good detective, but sometimes he didn't see the obvious. *Ain't it clear?* Brady thought, *Neil's not working here to win* Good Housekeeping's *Seal of Approval.*

"And when did you marry Mrs. Neil?" he asks David Neil.

"September 4, 1957." A light veneer of perspiration forms on the man's forehead, and a drop of it inches toward his temple.

The wife, Isabella, is recuperating in a private room at Roosevelt Hospital. The head injuries she sustained from the attack were simple lacerations. *Mostly frightened,* Brady thinks. Young and pretty—and five or six months pregnant—and scared out of her wits. *I'd be pretty frightened too,* Brady admits, picturing the suspect, her blonde hair concealed by a black wig, wielding a hammer above the victim's head.

Fifty-two years after my mother was arrested for assaulting Isabella Neil, I talk with Detective Edward T. Brady. He is almost eighty, but remembers the case "as if it were yesterday," certain he interviewed David Neil not in his office at *Good Housekeeping,* but at the West Fifty-Fourth Street precinct. Only one newspaper article about the crime, appearing in the *Daily News,* reveals where Neil was interviewed, and in their reporting, he was at work.

"The sad part of it," Brady tells me, "was that everybody involved was hurt." The Neil woman, he explains, was hospitalized because she was pregnant, not because of serious injury.

"I think she was hit with a glancing blow," he says. "As far as I can remember, I don't recall seeing any bandages on her head."

Not long after the assault, I tell him, the Neils divorced. "I didn't know that," he says. "As quick as the case came into my life, it went out."

"They dropped the charges," I say, "because they were scared of my mother." I say this as if I've spoken with both David and Isabella, but I haven't. All I have to go by are the court documents and newspaper articles recording this crime and the subsequent legal aftermath. In fact, I cannot locate the Neils. Even in this age of Internet investigative tools, apart from the short article in the *New York Times* about this violent day in the life of Isabella, these particular Neils do not come up when I Google their names; all the other newspapers that carried the story are either defunct or not electronically archived. Isabella would be almost eighty, David several years older, their child about my age. If, of course, they are all still alive.

What would I ask if I found them? "Remember that day in 1958 when a strange woman came to your door? That was my mother—would you mind answering a few questions?" Or, "Hi, David. My mother was that crazy woman you were dating in California. What can you tell me about her?" Or, "Did your parents ever tell you the story of what happened to your mom, before you were born, back in the late fifties?"

I *am* curious. Sometimes I think that if I had money, I'd pay someone to locate the Neils. But I am equally content to not interrupt their privacy. All that remains of my mother are the stories I tell about her; the instinct to cobble together a whole person of these pieces drives me to return, over and over again, to the narrative scraps with which I am familiar of Dolores's life. To imagine in their entirety the events that shape a life, in particular the life of the woman who gave you yours, is tantalizing, especially when no one is left to answer questions, and you realize that everything you discover, not to mention all you never knew and have to imagine, about your mother and father, especially once they are both dead, seems loaded with meaning. Though I'm not sure I'll decode any encrypted information that will illuminate once and for all the shadow that has become my mother, the chance of catching a glimpse of her true self lures me back. There is, too, the question of her identity, the great pains she took to ensure that no one, not even her only daughter, would ever really know who she was, and the lingering, if ever so fractional, possibility that I'll stumble upon some iota of information that will clarify everything and make sense of the things Dolores did, including trying to hurt a pregnant woman who married a man my mother had once loved.

"I met the Neil woman only once," Ed Brady says. "But I remember she told me she had been suspicious from the moment she opened the door." *Who wouldn't be?* I think. A stranger in a big city rings the doorbell and asks to use the phone. If you're gracious and perhaps a bit naïve, you let her in, even if you're skeptical. If you're mean spirited—and, some might argue, self-preserving—you tell her where the nearest pay phone is located.

"Do you remember," Ed Brady asks, "the plastic circles inside the dials of old telephones?" I immediately visualize the apartment I lived in as a kid during the 1970s. There is my father's armchair; next to it a table dominated by the phone, and in the center of that unwieldy appliance is a plastic disk that protects a circular piece of paper upon which is written, with blue ink and in my father's slightly slanted print, our home phone number, LE 5 6759.

The image of the telephone, with its curves and circles, materializes and dissolves, replaced with recollections that surface and fade as quickly, of the tittering conversations with boys I enjoyed on that apparatus. Brady explains that when he arrived at the scene of the crime, he noticed a photograph of Isabella under the plastic circle inside the Neil's phone. And when he says this, I see my mother's avocado-green telephone from the 1960s, a picture of her two Chihuahuas, Pepé and Candy, inside the circle, their ears disproportionately large.

According to the victim, the perpetrator had not only asked to use the phone, she pretended to be talking to someone once she held the receiver to her ear, though she was, Brady figured when he saw that telephone, probably faking the conversation and studying the image of Mr. Neil's lovely wife.

Brady tells me that after the attack on Isabella, David Neil was concerned whether they should move. "He was questioning me about how quickly I could identify who did this, and I told him, 'I think you know who did it better than me.'"

Then came the uncomfortable silence, the kind a good detective knows will force a suspect or witness to drop their guard.

"That's when I asked him, 'Is this a habit in your life, putting the pictures of the women in your life in your phone?'"

Perhaps it isn't in David Neil's office, but in Manhattan's Eighteenth Precinct where Ed Brady and David Neil sit in a busy room. The scene plays out in black and white, cigarettes burning, phones ringing, the sound of keys and locks, the smell of stale coffee insinuated in the film-noir atmosphere. At any moment, Barbara Stanwyck or Robert Mitchum might walk through the door.

"Yes, detective. Why do you ask?" Neil says.

"Tell me the names of the women whose pictures you put in your phone."

Which is when, Ed Brady tells me, my mother's name was mentioned.

III. *"love's characters come face to face."*

April 7, 1958, late morning

From his briefcase, David Neil removes a folder.

"This came two days before we were married," he says, handing the young detective a piece of paper. A telegram.

Ed Brady, a graduate of Fordham University, married with young children and living in Queens, who will be on the job and then work security until he retires, notes the date, September 2, 1957. What chaos must have ensued, he wonders, during the forty-eight hours before David Neil took Isabella to be his lawful wedded wife? He thinks about the normal commotion of weddings, the in-laws, the complaints, all the things that break or don't work and need repair, the people who don't show up, the ones who arrive unexpectedly. Add this complication, an ex-fiancée spurned, clearly the hell-hath-no-fury sort, and all Ed Brady can imagine are accusations about infidelity, arguments about jealousy, apologies, and promises signed with flowers. Boxes of expensive chocolates and conciliatory kisses. He reads the telegram: "I love you. Don't get married. Let's talk it over." Signed Dolores Buxton. He wonders why Neil saved this document.

"Dolores and I were sort of...well, I guess you'd say we were engaged," Neil tells Brady. "But she must have been out of her mind to send that wire." A bead of sweat disperses into his hairline. He takes a handkerchief from his jacket pocket and presses it, almost delicately, Brady notes, to his forehead. "It's so warm today," he says.

"I hadn't noticed," Brady says, though he is relieved that the rain has finally ended. The city practically flooded yesterday, on Easter Sunday no less. *What a mess that was*, he thinks. He sets down the telegram. "We'll have to keep this," he says, nodding toward the piece of paper. "Evidence."

"Of course," David Neil says. He rests his hands palms up on his trousered thighs, then turns them over, as if, Ed Brady thinks, to make sure his wedding band is very visible. "I love my wife, detective," Neil says.

And why not? Brady thinks. The man seems earnest enough, though Brady knows sincerity isn't the glue that keeps a marriage together. And this guy is a looker. "A regular Roam-e-o," Hanford had remarked.

"I have loved her ever since we met," Neil says, a little too self-consciously, Brady thinks, wondering as he looks at this well-groomed man how Dolores Buxton might have known the couple's unpublished address.

The two men sit in a silence punctuated by the sounds of a magazine office: telephones ringing, high heels clicking, typewriters clacking. Or, they sit in a silence disrupted by the sounds of a police precinct: doors opening and closing, coffee pouring, lighters snapping.

"The Neil woman," Ed Brady tells me, "was pretty much on her toes—and that's what probably saved her." When she described the perpetrator, she told police that the woman "wore a babushka on her head, and underneath it was black hair." Isabella Neil suspected the woman was wearing a wig because, as she told Brady, "her makeup wasn't the makeup a brunette would wear."

My mother, a cosmetics industry executive, the queen of disguise—why had she neglected to pay attention to her makeup? Is this the kind of detail that trumps all the circumstantial evidence pointing to her guilt, or does it elicit instead the kind of rushed rage inherent in a crime of passion, a rage that makes you forget to leave no trace?

And why was my mother so angry that she used a hammer to harm a pregnant woman, the day after Easter Sunday no less, a holiday that was a big deal for Dolores, who was half Catholic?

The story of my mother as a rejected, hell-hath-no-fury lover would be unknown to me were it not for the newspaper articles recounting her alleged attack of Isabella, the "slender redhead," as the reporters called her. She never talked about how it felt to be snubbed by David Neil, though she told me several times a story about being framed for a crime. Dolores was twenty-eight at the time, pursuing a successful career, on her way to fulfilling her dreams. The only piece missing in her life, as far as I can tell, was the courtship and subsequent relationship with Mr. Right, that iconic husband-hero of the 1950s, an almost urban legend of a man, depicted in the movies, advertising, pulp fiction, and ushered into the minds of girls and women by friends and co-workers, mothers, sisters, aunts, and grandmothers.

I find it impossible to inhabit Dolores's interior landscape on the morning of April seventh—too many details and variables detain me at the entrance to that troubled place. That she chose to wear a costume—the wig and the white uniform—tells me the crime was planned. Had she slept the night before? What do you dream of, if you dream, in the early morning hours before a premeditated assault? When had she decided to eliminate David Neil's new wife? Did my mother eat breakfast that morning or was hunger absent because of the flood of adrenaline that surely propelled her into putting a hammer in her handbag and taking care to disguise herself? She knew where the Neils lived[‡]—does that mean she had talked with David and learned his wife was expecting? Or had she followed him home after work? Perhaps they had renewed their affair, though it is unlikely that David plotted to hurt his wife, especially given that not long after the crime, he stood before the district attorney with Isabella, from whom he was divorced, pleading with the DA to drop the charges because, he said, they were scared of the defendant, who had since married my father but was capable, David Neil pointed out, of being quite vicious.

[‡] They are not listed in the city directory for 1957 or 1958.

IV. *"To be stripped of every fiction except one"*

April 7, 1958, morning

David Neil leaves for the office. His pregnant wife, Isabella, a former dress model, washes and dries the breakfast dishes. She wipes her hands and from an apron pocket takes a tube of lipstick, Elizabeth Arden's cyclamen, which she uncaps and applies. Though she expects no visitors, she will be leaving soon to shop, and in 1958, no woman working in the fashion business leaves her home without a fresh application of lip color. Isabella sits down at the table to write her list. But first, she looks at the April issue of *Good Housekeeping*, whose cover features a little girl gazing at a yellow duckling. The child wears a robin's-egg-blue dress with a scalloped, white collar, a matching blue ribbon in her red hair, her hand on her chin. Perhaps, she thinks, her baby will grow up to look like this girl. She meant to ask her husband if he was at the cover shoot or if he met the little girl but she kept forgetting. She pushes the magazine aside and is writing the word *milk* on the paper when the doorbell rings.

Contemplating this day later, she might recall thinking she had waddled to the door of her fourth-floor apartment at 345 West Fifty-Eighth Street, though she would wonder if it was the image of the duckling that made her think this; after all, Isabella had been trained to walk with assured elegance. She might also remember the regret she felt for having opened that door, for neglecting the American urban dweller's practice of squinting one eye and peering through the Judas hole, for not refusing entry to the woman with black hair, dark eyes, and very fair skin, dressed in white, wearing a gray-and-green head kerchief, a topcoat draped over one arm. A woman whose makeup was not right.

Mrs. Neil opens the door in what she perhaps will describe later to her friends, and maybe even to her child, as a gracious gesture. She is, after all, a cordial woman, married to a magazine executive, expected to entertain, to be possessed of flawless manners and carriage. To appear as if she were not an immigrant.

"I live upstairs," the stranger says. "May I use your telephone? Mine is out of order." Before Isabella can say yes or no, the woman enters. The two women look at one another for an instant before Isabella leads her to the living room and guides her toward a round table, recently polished.

"Please," Isabella says with her faint German accent, "by all means use the phone."

In the center of the dial is a black-and-white photo of Mrs. Neil. Taken before the pregnancy, she is barely twenty in the picture. The chic Dior dress emphasizes her wasp waist. Her hair, makeup, and nails are impeccable.

Isabella tries not to eavesdrop, but she hears the woman say some words into the receiver, pause, and say more words. Later, Isabella does not recall the words, though there was something odd about the tone, something that seemed just slightly off. But as the stranger talks into the phone, Isabella chides herself silently—the nuances of English are sometimes indecipherable to her. She dismisses any suspicion of oddity, suspending her disbelief a little further when the woman tells Isabella she works in television.

"I'm looking for pregnant women to appear on certain programs," the woman says. "But perhaps we can discuss this another time. May I use your powder room?"

Isabella gestures toward the bathroom. After a minute or so, she hears the toilet flush and the door open.

"There's a problem in here," the woman says. "The toilet is leaking."

Isabella approaches. "I don't see any water," she says.

"It's on the other side," the stranger says.

Isabella Neil, cornered in her own bathroom, watches as the woman takes from her handbag a hammer, which she raises above Isabella's head. But the assailant is clumsy, or maybe simply unpracticed, and instead of hitting Isabella, the first blow strikes a decorative louver in the bathroom, nicking the wood, and afterward grazes Isabella's skull. The redheaded mother-to-be feels as if she might faint, but instead she urges herself up and manages to flee from the bathroom, only to be pursued by the perpetrator, who has returned the hammer to her purse and is now using a small Mexican statuette from a table in the living room to continue her assault.

"Don't call the police," the attacker warns, trying to stuff a gag into Isabella's mouth, leaving the scene of the crime after Isabella bites the stranger's gloved finger.

While she may not have recalled the exact words her assailant had said earlier into the telephone, Isabella, one must imagine, never forgot the comingled taste of leather and blood.

———————

I once saw a fight between two young women, in front of New York City's Penn Station. A crowd had gathered, its members gasping collectively as one of the fighters broke from a policeman's hold, and threw a straightforward punch to the victim's face before jumping on her and continuing to slap and hit, seemingly unstoppable until three cops intervened and handcuffed her. During the assault, the air around the scene had become statically charged, heavy with the scent of the primal human, something I felt at the one and only professional heavyweight boxing match I ever attended.

But being a bystander at a street brawl or the spectator at a prizefight is completely unlike knowing that your mother was the offender of a violent crime. The rage that propelled Dolores is not only part of who she was, it belongs to me as well, surfacing when I am faced with situations that anger me—bureaucracies such as health-insurance companies or corporations, or my neighbor killing a snake because he thinks they don't deserve to live under his porch, the nausea of television and politics, the daily tectonic shifts at home or work that feel like caustic betrayals, even though they're really only minor misunderstandings, arguments, resentments, impatience. I have felt the heat of fury rise from my groin and watched—as if I were outside my own body as it occurs—the erasure of all trace of composure, rationality, and compassion as I slam a door and then sob uncontrollably, ashamed of myself, praying to die on the spot. I've been overwhelmed by ignorance or apathy and wanted to break plates, but this is the kind of rage everyone feels, at least once. For a period of time in my thirties, I was trapped in a violent relationship, and the captivity and fear so enraged me one night that, after a jealous tirade by the man who supposedly loved me, I shredded a portrait of me painted by a friend, to prove, perhaps, that only I could hurt myself more than he could.

My mother taught me that strategy, and later it became clear to me that she was unable to move on from wanting to hurt herself as a response to things that went wrong. She chose with purpose to carry out the battering of a stranger, a woman more vulnerable than she. As Dolores aged, she turned this violence inward, on herself. The timing—both crimes occurred just after Easter Sunday—could not have been a coincidence.

I have spent a good part of my adolescence and adulthood denying I am anything like the woman who gave me life, a mother described as unfit by the courts, a drug-addicted liar, a criminal; a woman so depressed she took her own life. Yet such refusal is not only unproductive, it renders sterile any chance of making meaning. To be a relation is, in the purest sense of the word *relate*, to carry back. I *am* my mother's daughter: in my use of makeup and hair color to disguise imperfections and age, in my departures into darkness and failures at intimacy, in my order and control of the physical world around me lest the disorder unground me, I carry Dolores—and her sorrow, which curdled into regret and then anger—back to life. The blood Isabella tasted that day carried the genetic source material now occupying my cells. I have used illegal drugs, not always told the truth, shoplifted, considered ending my life, and once, many years ago, was disproportionately angry at my dog. If confessing these acts makes me nervous, then how might Dolores have felt when she faced herself, alone, in the still darkness of 3:00 am, when no one was available, least of all some gentler version of herself, to pardon her transgressions?

What if I had been more available to her in those last months? How might I have turned out differently had I forgiven her then or visited more often or convinced her to tell the truth? I can hardly imagine my mother and me in a relationship unburdened by tension; our kinship was limned at the murky edges of things such as the leveling at dusk of the will and the melancholy of dirty snow. Nor can I feel how I might have felt had I been a different daughter; one who had listened to her story about being framed for a crime she hadn't committed; one who asked her questions, probing for the truth; one who, in seeing the truth, was able to still hold her mother's hand and honestly say that she absorbed the *why* if not the what of her unraveling.

V. *"Life's nonsense pierces us with strange relation."*

April 7, 1958, afternoon

"If the attacker hadn't been wearing a glove," Isabella Neil told Ed Brady, "I'd have bitten off her finger because I bit so hard." Which makes the encounter between the two women sound more and more like an edging-out-of-control cat fight, a term my mother surely despised because it reduces the rage quotient inherent in her act to an event that transforms humans into felines and charges—electrically—those who view such angered performance from its periphery. And for my mother, the stereotypical cat fight probably connoted the barroom brawl in which two women, passions enflamed by drink, sparred. Such quarrels likely recalled for her a childhood wrought of anything but privilege, a childhood spent moving from one place to another because of her father's illegal hustles, a childhood she had tried desperately to escape by aspiring to a lifestyle that transcended her origins.

After David Neil informed Ed Brady about his past relationship with Dolores Buxton, the detective went to the suspect's apartment at 231 East Seventy-Sixth Street. "She really had no alibi," he tells me. According to court records, my mother told the detective she arrived late, 10:00 am, to work, "owing to an attack of diarrhea." But the switchboard operator at Dolores's office stated she had received a telephone call from the defendant after ten on the morning of the crime and that Dolores Buxton had told her she had overslept and would be arriving late to the office that day.

"She had a bandage on her finger," Ed Brady says. "When I asked her what had happened, she told me she dropped a typewriter on it."

Ed Brady, whose eyes are clear and whose voice never falters, continues speaking, though my mind is stuck contemplating the frequency of injuries to the forefinger from falling typewriters.

"I asked her if she had any tools," Ed Brady continues. "She said no. I asked her if she had a junk drawer, but when I opened it, no hammer there. But then I looked under the sink and I found a hammer."

What was she thinking? I wonder.

Ed Brady remembers the burr in the hammer's head as well as the mark it left on the decorative louver in Isabella Neil's bathroom. And even though the district attorney's recommendation for discharge reveals that the laboratory could not "state conclusively that the hammer found in the defendant's apartment was the weapon used in the assault," I surmise that this detective, even now, so long after the crime, felt fairly certain of the prime suspect's guilt when he discovered the hammer, which still had traces of human blood on it, beneath my mother's kitchen sink.

Neither Ed Brady nor any of the newspaper reporters mention the discovery of what was worn by the attacker— the wig, the green-and-white scarf, the white dress, white stockings, and white shoes—which provides me respite, albeit brief, of reasonable doubt concerning my mother's guilt. But I also know that she had plenty of time to return home after the attack and dispose of the disguise.

Roosevelt Hospital, at Fifty-Ninth Street and Tenth Avenue, is familiar to me because my mother was hospitalized there when I was a girl. But on the day Dolores was brought to Isabella Neil's room by detectives Brady and Hanford, the hospital was just another building in a series of buildings that my mother entered and exited, and because she was so newly transplanted in Manhattan, in all likelihood, the afternoon of April 7, 1958, marked her first visit there.

In some ways, that's all a city is—a succession of diverse architectures, some more elegant than others, some more functional, some more dreary, some more apt to be condemned, all of them the setting for some performance of one kind or another, all of them equipped with doors that one must open and close in a never-ending cycle of entry and egress. In 1958, Dolores lived at 231 East Seventy-Sixth Street. "A luxury apartment building," Ed Brady calls it, emphasizing the word luxury when we speak five-plus decades after my mother lived there. Today, though a sign outside its entrance still advertises Luxury Apartments, nothing recommends the building as a dwelling of any specific opulence.

Here in this eight-story red brick building, built in 1937 as a convent, across the street from the Robert Wagner School, and only several blocks away from Lenox Hill Hospital (where she would deliver her only child just eighteen months later), Dolores Eleanor Buxton, who should have been going to work Monday morning, prepared herself to commit a crime that would secure her passage on an ever-accelerating undoing. And yet, I wonder, had she erased this pivotal day from her itinerary, would my mother have plummeted anyway?

Picture the charge nurse at Roosevelt Hospital that April day: she has the bad luck to have been working the shift that started on Easter Sunday, one of the wettest days in recent memory, with all kinds of accidents coming through the ER, and all manner of rain-induced ailments, from colds to pneumonia. And here it is Monday, the storms finally over, and in comes the pretty pregnant woman. Five, six months along. Jittery, with a lacerated scalp. Someone had tried to hit her about the head with a blunt object, but as far as anyone can tell, she is mostly suffering from a case of shock.

Several hours after the woman is admitted, in walk the trio—two men, obviously cops, escorting a curvy blonde. *Nothing but trouble here*, thinks the nurse. She has seen everything there is to see inside a hospital—birth, death, crime, wounds, disease, passion, but never someone attacking an expectant mother. *An intolerable crime.*

"Gentlemen?" she asks. Her voice stops men cold.

"We're here for Mrs. Isabella Neil," one of them says. He reaches into his pocket and pulls out his detective's shield.

"She's resting now, officers," the nurse says, watching the blonde shift her gaze from the floor to the exit beyond the desk. She isn't a natural blonde, though her hair is fashionably curled, and, the nurse thinks, the woman would be quite attractive if she didn't look so...trapped, if she weren't wearing the strange combination of a horizontally striped overcoat and a modestly collared dress, if her clothing wasn't saturated with the stale smell of cigarette smoke.

"Mrs. Neil has to identify a potential suspect," one of the detectives says.

The blonde, whom the other officer is gripping, squirms a bit and grimaces. She is the third woman they've brought in today.

I've seen it all now, the charge nurse thinks, shaking her head and leading the three down the corridor toward the room where the pretty young pregnant woman, *who has had enough for today,* the nurse wants to tell these cops, is trying to recover.

Jack Hanford pushes open the door; Ed Brady guides Dolores Buxton by the arm into the room. Perhaps Isabella Neil is awake, and David, playing the role of the ever-attentive husband, sits in a chair and leans toward her.

And what are the expectant parents discussing before this interruption? Did the idea of divorce already coalesce in Isabella's mind, despite David's pleas to forgive him his prior involvement with a crazy and violent woman? Or did the notion of sundering their union hatch when Isabella sees, as the door opens, how Dolores and David look at one another, with, if not tenderness, an unmistakable magnetism? Or did the thirty-year-old promotions manager at *Good Housekeeping* simply assure his former-dress-model wife that everything was going to be okay?

The two detectives each hold one of Dolores's arms. Isabella shrinks back on the hospital bed.

"That's her!" she screams.

———————

Ed Brady tells me that after my mother was arrested, she was taken to a precinct on Manhattan's East Side, "where they kept women," and arraigned the next morning. "She probably spent the night there," he explains, "unless she was bailed out." I'm not sure, however, that this is what happened exactly. According to a Daily News article that appeared the next day—referred to in a report compiled by Bishop's Service, Inc., an investigative firm hired by my father's divorce attorney—Dolores was not released. A hearing was scheduled for April 17; court records indicate that a grand jury indicted her on May 1, 1958, for felonious assault and burglary. Her bail bond of $1,000 was issued on May 7, 1958.

After my mother died, I discovered chapters and proposals she had drafted for two books, which each told variations of the "nonfiction story" of one Brandy Olin Dunhill, a fictionalized version of Dolores. In each, the narrative begins during Brandy's incarceration—"for a crime she did not commit"—at a facility on Riker's Island. The detectives in the Neil case, the newspapers covering the story of the crime, and the private investigators hired by my father's lawyer later in 1965 never mention another assault connected to my mother, which makes me wonder if she was actually sent to a correctional facility for several weeks after her arrest for the assault of Isabella Neil.

Riker's Island did not house female inmates in 1958. My mother probably went to the Women's House of Detention, the art-deco, fortress-like structure that stood at 10 Greenwich Avenue from 1931 to 1974 and was around the corner from 15 Charles Street, where we lived for a brief time during the sixties, just before moving to West Seventieth Street. My mother started writing about her alter ego Brandy in the early 1980s; by that time, the infamous and much criticized Women's House of Detention had been demolished, replaced with the Jefferson Market Garden. But why didn't my mother simply write the story when and where it really took place?

My mother constructed untruths about nearly everything, though in her duplicity some form of the truth usually surfaced, if you knew what to listen or look for as she spun her various and mythically charged autobiographies. That's the short answer; the more complex one concerns her refusal—perhaps *inability* is the more accurate word— to see herself for who she was, in spite of all those hours spent in front of or in service to the mirror. Or, put another way, a part of my mother probably needed to analyze her actions and those of others while disconnecting, though her accounts consistently cast Brandy Olin Dunhill into the role of a suave and highly intelligent sophisticate who is duped and victimized by rich and powerful men. Which is so two-dimensional and trite, qualities that the real Dolores, a self-educated and ahead-of-her-times woman, would have disdained had she been able to step back and scrutinize the character she had projected onto herself.

In April 1958, my mother worked for the Glenby Corporation, whose offices were located at 120 East Sixteenth Street, the same address provided by one Emanuel Finkelstein, the attorney listed on my mother's bail bond. The authors of the Bishop's report note that Dolores "was employed for the purpose of promoting a diet reducing pill or pills at beauty salon concessions maintained by Glenby Corporation at various department stores."

None of this is mentioned in my mother's unfinished "nonfiction" narrative. Instead, the version Dolores crafted of herself was a celebrity elite who is thrown into a criminal milieu that impoverishes her: in the draft chapter that begins in Riker's, a prison psychiatrist finds a severely beaten, raped woman whom he recognizes immediately as Brandy Olin Dunhill because she had appeared "less than a month previous, on the *Dinah Shore Show*" and was endowed, he recalls, with "looks, brains, personality, fame, money—everything." The detail of the *Dinah Shore Show*[##] and the major discrepancy between my mother's experience and her rendering of it, that women were not taken to Riker's until after the demolition of the Women's House of Detention in 1974, alert me to the possibility that my mother, who was writing her story three decades after the assault on Isabella Neil, probably was incarcerated and suffered humiliation and/or violence while in detention in the late 1950s.

More than fifty years later and I still don't know what to make of this story except that the truth of my mother is hidden somewhere within it, and that even she had lost the thread of what was real and what was pretend. In a moment of frustration with me when I was a girl who clung to her mother's stories, my father opened his filing cabinet and dug out the newspaper articles documenting my mother's alleged assault of Isabella Neil, in an attempt to persuade me that Dolores, the fourth of his six wives, was not the white-picket-fence mother she professed to be but was, rather, an imposter. Ever since that day, I have vacillated between finding my mother guilty and having reasonable doubt. I was ten years old when my father handed me the folder containing those Photostatted copies. The allegiance I professed to my mother at that time—a loyalty that could tip the scales of family-court justice—pushed my father into

---

[##] And became the *Dinah Shore Chevy Show* in 1957 and aired until 1963.

unlocking that drawer to show me those artifacts, which were, even he knew, not proof of her guilt.

That no solid answers are forthcoming leads me to various speculations, though I do admit the certain weight of what is known as a legal fiction, "an assumption of a possibility as a fact, irrespective of the question of its truth," which is itself

fabricated (the word *fiction*, not surprisingly, comes from the Latin for fashion) from court records, journalistic accounts, a detective's recollection, my mother's invented stories, and my own imagination. I may be the archivist of my mother's story and the one person alive who knows more about her than anyone else, but like the hairdresser in the Miss Clairol hair-color ads, only Isabella Neil "knew for sure." Such uncertainty increases the fictional quality of Dolores, which may also explain why I have had such a vested interest in solving this particular puzzle. After all, if she is a made-up character in a drama with no distinct conclusion, what does that make me?

DAY 4:

A Duet of Shade and Light

Most people are other people. Their thoughts are someone else's opinions, their lives a mimicry, their passions a quotation.

—*Oscar Wilde, De Profundis*

Forgive me that I ignored the sun
And that I lived in sorrow.
Forgive, forgive, that I
Mistook too many others for you.

—*Anna Akhmatova, Spring 1915 trans. by W. S. Merwin*
[March 19, 1953]

I. "she still clutches / the copper wafer, the fee for the misty crossing."

Dolores Eleanor Buxton kept two secrets: her true age and her real name. In these times, she told herself, what with accusations about being un-American, and the Rosenbergs on trial, one had to stretch a fact here and there. What Dolores told no one is that she experienced a kind of freedom when she told her so-called little white lies, a liberation from the life she believed had been scripted for her. This sensation of release led her at first to dream up alternate realities, then in turn seduced her into embroidering real-life stories with snippets of fiction (a quirk that made her a coveted guest at parties), and resulted, once the art of living with or among others no longer interested her, in an elaborate labyrinth of deception, a maze so convoluted even Dolores could no longer identify the starting point. Besides, as she once confided to a friend, every time she tried to tell the truth, no one believed her.

On the morning of Thursday, March 19, 1953, just two and a half months shy of twenty-three (twenty-four if you knew her real age), Dolores examined her face in the mirror, first the left side, then the right. She gave no thought to the approaching vernal equinox; seasons only interested Dolores in terms of fashion; she had no inclination for farming or stargazing. She scrutinized her eyebrows and plucked a stray hair, noted with a barely audible yet satisfied sigh the absence of blemishes on her skin, and stopped short of telling herself that her eyes were too dark. *What good does it do to wish they were another color?* she thought. Then, as she did every morning, she proceeded to put on her face. Had someone been watching her, the ritual application of foundation, blush, eyebrow pencil, eye shadow, eyeliner, mascara, and lipstick might have appeared more like prayer: Dolores's attention to her reflection was absolute, as if she were before an altar, and, if not beholding a sacred image, at least gazing upon what she imagined was the semblance of one.

No surprise then, that in such an enraptured state, Dolores happened upon an idea so stunning it made her gasp. The moment seemed illuminated. Even Pepé, her Chihuahua, looked up from his wicker basket near her feet. Ever prepared, she pulled away her hand before it wiggled, set down the eyeliner brush, and picked up a pencil.

"Mirror, mirror, on the wall," she wrote in a distinctive, willowy cursive practiced late into the night and praised by every teacher from Newark, New Jersey, to Portland, Oregon, whose classrooms she had visited as if they were different departments in a large store (her father, after all, had been a "traveling salesman," though not the kind with a sample case and worn shoes). "Who's the fairest of them all?" she asked aloud.

She set down the pencil, patted Pepé's head, lit a cigarette, and pondered her idea. She took two pulls on the unfiltered Chesterfield, left it to burn in the ashtray, and turned her complete concentration to the pad, an item she had placed on the table in anticipation of exactly this sort of inspirational moment. On it she sketched a full-length oval mirror and the slightly bulky figure of a generic woman standing before the glass. Inside the mirror, Dolores drew a svelte version of the woman. On the bottom of the page, she printed the words *Magic Mirror*. She loved mixing together the good and bad from the Snow White fairytale—the vanity of the evil queen and the innocence and everydayness of the eternal virgin (and more importantly, her prematernity figure and youthful good looks)—to lure women into purchasing their own transformation. She would find someone to design and manufacture the magic mirror. She would sell it. Dolores shut her eyes and pictured women standing before the looking glass, delighted with the reflection of themselves less those ten to fifteen pounds they struggled to shed year after year to no avail. Ten pounds wasn't so much—the weight of a small turkey, two bags of groceries, an infant—but it imprisoned some women. And, Dolores thought, she was going to set them free, allow them to see a seemingly real image of a body from which a subtraction had been made. Such a promise of renewal would motivate them to follow a regimen of diet and exercise. As part of the package, a trained dietician would counsel them about nutrition, and a guru like Jack LaLanne would develop a plan for their physical fitness. And she, Dolores, would direct this entire enterprise, having earned for herself that corner office on Madison Avenue, a secretary, a chauffeur. She imagined opening a closet filled with an entire wardrobe from Saks.

She stubbed out the cigarette and picked up the eyeliner brush. All her daydreams were a welcome distraction from the exigencies of the life she was living, which was devoted to cornering a particular part of the cosmetics market, days and evenings spent in high heels and tight undergarments, a life whose chief result was an odd mix of deprivation ("You can't stay thin eating all the foods you like," she often told herself) and overindulgence (ten products for the face alone). Dolores, whose early childhood was defined by the Depression, knew intimately the deprivation part. She craved the excess. As proof of her faith in this modern religion, she currently spent more money on beauty than on food. Even the dog, a black-and-white short-coated Chihuahua, seemed an extravagance. Pepé had been a gift from her father, and though she appreciated the animal's company, humorous antics, and unconditional adoration, she also knew that people were more inclined to trust you if you had a dog. Her father, Buxie, who had two Chihuahuas in tow at all times, had taught her that.

Dolores finished her makeup application with the same quick, deft strokes she had used to sketch the magic mirror. Her face, she knew, was her chief asset: on that perfect oval resided a set of large, dark brown eyes framed by brows tweezed into dramatic, horizontal parentheses; a nose that had been surgically shaped to be ethnically unidentifiable; and a mouth whose upper and lower lips were full and which she kept precisely lined and fully lipsticked at all times. Her skin was without flaw, her hair swept up and curled on top of her head, her neck long. The colors, lines, and shadows she had just added to her face emphasized the legacy of beauty that she had come to take for granted. A beauty, she said later, that hurt.

She dressed in a no-nonsense outfit—a simple white silk blouse, a tan-and-brown-checked pencil skirt, stockings, plain leather pumps.

"A corner office and a closet full of Saks are all well and good, Pepé," she said, "but now I need to go to work." She checked the contents of her pocketbook, took stock of her face one last time in the mirror, and headed toward the front door of the apartment. Before taking her raincoat from the closet, she removed from her purse money for Cora, the woman who, every Thursday, cleaned the house and shopped for groceries. Dolores jotted down a few items on a list, folded it around the cash, and slid this packet into an envelope, which she set in the open palm of the Greek goddess statue near the door.

Her job involved the hiring, training, and supervision of prospective employees—figure analysts and salon attendants—at the growing franchise of Slenderella salons. Dolores was familiar with using fairytales to market beauty.

"Inside every woman is the possibility of Cinderella," she told the new hires, who were pretty young women with dreams of their own. "She is the princess waiting to be discovered, whose transformation is possible when her true potential is realized." It is not just a job, she reminded them, rather it is a vocation to offer salon patrons the opportunity to imagine the beautiful woman hidden by the weight they had gained and then educate them as to how to find and maintain her.

"Never tell them they are going to *lose weight*," Dolores instructed the trainees. "Instead, use the word *slenderize*." Of course, part of the regime that unlocked and released their secret loveliness included a minimum of thirty ("Though we recommend one hundred or more for best results") forty-five-minute sessions on a vibrating, white-leatherette-padded table set up in a curtained booth. The cost: two dollars a session, with a 10 percent discount for cash payments made in advance.

"Never say *up front*," Dolores cautioned them.

As for the man behind all this, Larry Mack, Dolores thought he was a hustler. She was familiar with the appeal and intelligence of the confidence man, her father being the first one she had ever known (the traveling-salesman euphemism dropped long ago), and, in all fairness, to whom she owed a lot of her business smarts. And even though Mack had secured the endorsement of the reputable Dr. Fishbein from the Chicago Department of Health, Dolores knew that deprivation and hard work, not those silly tables, achieved results. The figure analysts and attendants—all of them trim, attractive, well coiffed and unblemished, educated, tactful, well mannered, and good with people—served as motivation. Replace them and the tables with magic mirrors, Dolores thought, and you eliminated an enormous overhead cost.

"Call you a taxi, Miss Buxton?" asked the doorman, standing at attention in the lobby of 231 East Seventy-Sixth Street. Dolores knew he liked the way she smelled, the buoyant white of Ivory soap and the sticky-sweet hairspray, and, if he were to ever come close enough, the bare musk of Chanel No. 5 dabbed discreetly at the back of her neck.

"Yes, Harold," she said.

Harold stepped outside into the chilly morning while Dolores waited in the lobby. She appraised him through the lobby's plate-glass window. His stocky build was that of a man who, on a Saturday night, would take a girl to a cool Midtown joint—the kind that served steaks and chops. His date would wear a flouncy dress, something with lace or chiffon. A white patent-leather pocketbook and white gloves that buttoned at the wrists. She'd be the kind of woman who wore nylon, not silk, stockings with unembellished garters.

Dolores examined her silhouette in the lobby's mirror. Her full-length reflection always startled her a bit: at five-foot-nine, her bust proportionate to her hips, waist a mere twenty-four inches, she resembled her mother, though Dorothy's hair had been thick and black and long. Her mother would have been forty-four had she lived, Dolores thought, realizing with a chill she preferred not to acknowledge that today was the second anniversary of her mother's death.

Of course none of that mattered now. Dolores had a regular boyfriend, a tall man with thick hair, who dressed in expensive Italian suits and silk ties and wore a gold watch she had given him, engraved with a message promising her everlasting love. He enjoyed gimlets and Peggy Lee. A man who once worked out West with Buxie, Dolores's father, who had been, in fact, one of Stuart Buxton's protégés.

David Neil was the only man who called her Dolores, not Debbie, the nickname she had earned as a youngster because her initials spelled *Deb*. Nicknames unnerved Dolores; she saw laziness in the diminishing of nomenclature, took it as a sign that the world was moving toward an unadult place. The diminutive nature of pet names took away the meaning intended by parents when they bestowed a given name to a child. She did not appreciate the affection supposedly inherent in terms of endearment ("Daddy, *please* stop calling me Dizzy," she once pleaded with her father when she was nine, "I am *not* spinning"), and having grown up long before her childhood ended, she did not want to be cast as an eternal child.

The taxicab arrived. Harold opened the door and as he held it, the back of his white glove was visible, as was the coffee-colored stain, the size of a small freckle.

"Have a nice day, Miss Buxton," he said as she arranged her briefcase next to her on the car's seat and crossed her long and effortlessly shapely legs.

"And you, Harold," she said, smiling the way a fashion model smiles at everyone, as if her interest in the happiness of strangers was genuine. As if she hadn't seen the spot on the doorman's glove and wondered why he hadn't taken the time to have his work clothing properly laundered when she, Dolores Eleanor Buxton, devoted such absolute attention to everything she wore.

II. *"Vague as fog and looked for like mail."*

On Thursday mornings, Dolores met with Joan Grove, a supervisor of training personnel, in her Midtown office on Fifth Avenue. Then she made the rounds to the Slenderella salons in Manhattan, checking in with the managers, collecting the aptitude and personality tests administered to prospective hires, reviewing complaints about employees, awarding praise to those who had excelled. It seemed to Dolores that the women she worked with liked her, though she maintained a safe distance. Best, she thought, not to let anyone too close. With the exception of Cora, who towered over the tallest of men, whose single hand was larger than Pepé, and to whom Dolores felt an allegiance that afforded reciprocal generosity and confidentiality, women, she had decided, were not to be trusted. She worked hard to convince them that she was smarter than the most intelligent among them. In order to be believable, she had learned, boundaries had to be constructed and preserved. She was sure they all wanted her job. She was in charge of things, and, too, at such a young age.

As the taxi stopped and started through the city's morning traffic, Dolores thought back to January of 1951, when she and David had met in Los Angeles, several months before her mother had died.

One night David took her to the Villa Nova Club on Sunset Strip, where, he informed her, Joe DiMaggio and Marilyn Monroe went on their first spaghetti-dinner date. He ordered a gimlet and she an apricot sour. While they waited for their drinks, David said he wanted to meet her mother.

"Hasn't my father told you?" she had asked.

"Told me what?"

Dolores remembered how she might have been honest and told David that her mother was in the hospital, ravaged by a progressive and severe form of multiple sclerosis. She was, presently, dying. But the waiter came just then with their cocktails, and his arrival precipitated a pause in the conversation, a gap that lasted just long enough for her to imagine a different story about her mother. In that small moment, the truth evaporated. Realizing that Buxie hadn't told David the truth, she did not tell it either. Especially because she wouldn't have to explain why she had no intention of being there to help her mother through the illness or imminent death.

Instead, Dolores recalled now in the taxi, she had spun for David a tale that bore the stamp of quintessential 1950s America.

"My mother was institutionalized," she told him, then took a sip of her drink, pausing, watching David. She was waiting for that instant when information registers, a softening around the eyes, the lips parting slightly, the released but barely audible breath of acknowledgment. She let the pause swell. *Paranoid schizophrenia:* these words she said to herself, summoning the sour metal taste of the electricity she knew was used to treat such patients, and by so imbibing that mineral flavor, made herself believe, physically, the lie she had told, just as she did when she was telling it.

"She has paranoid schizophrenia," Dolores said as matter-of-factly as she could. "She's quite dangerous, in fact." She picked up her glass, took another sip, set it down. After that, the story flowed without any hesitation: she told David how her mother had killed one of Buxie's beloved Chihuahuas—drowned him in the bathtub, what a terrible mess *that* had been—and even tried to poison Buxie because she was convinced he was trying to frame her for a crime she didn't commit

"But, darling, you cannot speak of it with my father," she said. She lowered her voice to confide in David: Buxie, she told him, had remarried even though she knew he was still in love with her mother.

"And anyway, she doesn't recognize any of us," she had said, a final embellishment. "There's nothing anyone can do." This last remark she delivered in a half whisper.

He hadn't known what to say, Dolores realized as the cab stopped near the Plaza Hotel. She recalled how David had tilted his head slightly, pressed his lips together into a serious line, and looked her in the eye, his trademark expression of sympathy, learned, she later speculated, from observing puppies. He reached across the table and took her hand. And with that gesture, the man who up until then had been her date every other Saturday for the last two months became a serious prospect for a future husband. She knew she would follow David wherever he went.

"It must be so hard on you," he had said.

She assumed the role completely at that instant, mustering the teary-eyed look of the daughter exhausted by years of not knowing if her mother was going to be delusional from one day to the next.

"I've learned to manage," she said.

Of course, Dolores had learned so much more. Here she was, two years later, practically an executive, not yet twenty-five, her figure intact and name as yet untarnished. She had left California and the chatter of Buxie's orbit, was making it at a straight job, living in a luxury apartment building in Manhattan, where men opened doors for her and carried her bags. A dog greeted her each morning and evening with unparalleled affection. Her housekeeper was her confidante. A brand new television set provided entertainment right there in her living room. If she played her cards right, she'd maintain this life, sharing yet more luxuries with David once they married, a life many times removed from poverty (the cramped and underheated living quarters, cold water, shared toilets, the unending why-can't-we-have-that scarcity), fraud (the constant looking over one's shoulder, all the many moves to new homes in new cities in new states), and the petty resentments of Buxie's Old-World Jewish parents, who had been against the union of their son—they had envisioned him becoming a rabbi—to Dorothy, her Catholic mother.

III. *"To meet some new grief."*

"Light a candle, Dolores," her grandmother Margaret had written on March 19, 1951, the day Dorothy had died, the words penned in that flourished-yet-disciplined handwriting learned by young women who came of age in the nineteenth century, inked onto a halved piece of rose-scented linen stationery.

The instruction surfaced every several months in Dolores's mind, compelling her to enter the nearest church, where she deposited fifty cents in the donation box, kindled a devotional light, stood awkwardly before a figure of the Virgin Mary, and prayed to be forgiven for abandoning her mother. What good had it done? she wondered. In her private inventory of the things that brought relief from having lost the one person who had not only brought her into the world but who treated her with unconditional kindness, Dolores rated candle lighting as Not Very Effective, as well as a waste of hard-earned cash. *I should instead burn that note from my grandmother,* Dolores thought as the taxi stopped at 500 Fifth Avenue, where Joan Grove was waiting in her tenth-floor office.

"Folly *is* thrifty," the driver said.

"Excuse me?" Dolores asked.

"A dollar fifty, I said, Miss."

Dolores removed a glove and felt her forehead with the back of her hand. Her skin was cool, no hint of fever. Still, she was certain the driver had made that odd comment. She paid him and, as she started to collect her belongings, she noticed a small crucifix hanging from his rearview mirror. Dolores was unsure if it had been there when she first entered the taxi.

"Driver, do you know where the nearest Catholic church is?" she asked before she opened the door.

"St. Mary the Virgin," he said, "Forty-Sixth between Sixth and Seventh."

"Please take me there." She settled back into the cushiony leather and released her grip on the handle of the briefcase.

She knew the driver was looking at her in his rearview mirror long enough to articulate and then dismiss his first thought—*it's your nickel, lady*—and to instead commit to memory her face. She would be the passenger who changed her mind. When she first slid into the backseat, she had been all business. Now she wondered if she appeared a bit pale; she felt her facial muscles twitch ever so slightly.

As the cab pulled up to the church, Dolores was already reviewing the excuse she was going to make, one that Joan Grove, who insisted on punctuality and brevity, might believe: Unless traffic could be a real reason for tardiness, it was out of the question as others in the office might confirm or deny it. If Dolores said that she couldn't find a taxi, Joan would ask her why she didn't take a bus. Plumbing and electrical emergencies were equally fallible pretexts because they warranted a telephone call made to the office if they had really occurred. But a telephone call from an old friend who bent her ear with sad news (a relative who died, a mutual school chum who was ill), or a neighbor whose son was killed in Korea—now there were stories she could spin and which were, in the context of Joan Grove, unverifiable.

Dolores paid and thanked the driver. As she left the cab and walked up the steps to the doors of St. Mary the Virgin, she rehearsed her lie: "I'm so sorry I'm late, Miss Grove. My dearest friend from Rochester called with dreadful news about her father, who died yesterday in an accident." And in case Dolores had to answer any questions that Miss Grove might ask, she invented this story's details, which accumulated as the seconds ticked by: Sue was her friend; she lived on Gothic Street, just three doors down; Dolores had been like a second daughter to her friend's father, Melvin, who was driving to work—he was a chemistry teacher—when a truck hit him, head on; the funeral was to be held Sunday. Dolores was fond of calling such justifications "harmless little white lies." These you used, she later told her daughter—a child she could not, as she stood with her hand on the door of a Midtown sanctuary, imagine having—only when you *had* to conceal something that was both important and secret.

The interior of the church was, as she expected, quiet and cool, bringing Dolores as close to a cave as she would ever come. The damp stone smell, punctuated by the odor of burning candles, made her feel as if she were in a grotto that had been, somehow, relieved of its undergroundedness. She did not understand the allure of roadside-attraction caverns with their stalactites and stalagmites, or why anyone might spend a perfectly fine weekend *spelunking*. Even the word annoyed her. Dolores refused to put up with insects, burnt skin (and the aging caused by exposure to the sun), and dirt, especially when one lived in a grand metropolis like New York City, where you could procure everything you wanted, including a stroll or a carriage ride in Central Park, not only with great civility but with none of the side effects of going "to the country," as Manhattan dwellers called it. Such a dismissal of Nature, Dolores knew, represented an attitude that she attributed erroneously to landed gentry, who were not, decidedly, her people. Still, such ways of thinking accorded perfectly with the alteration of her name to Buxton, which was a refined and moneyed-sounding name.

At the base of the statue of the Virgin, in small blue glass jars, burned the familiar votive candles. A vase of daffodils and hyacinth had been placed at Mary's feet. Dolores studied the figure: her hands were raised in prayer, head covered, and neck sheathed as though she were a nun. Her long thin nose, unsmiling mouth, and eyes cast slightly downward made this Holy Virgin seem older and severe, inclined, perhaps, to be more reserved in her dispensation of mercy.

Dolores took a dollar bill from her purse, slipped it into the donation box, and lit two candles, one for each year that had passed since Dorothy had died.

"Holy Virgin," she whispered, "I left my mother, may she rest in peace, in her time of need. This was a mistake." Though she had been tempted to ask forgiveness, Dolores decided instead to simply admit the error, a strategy that assumed responsibility without implicating herself, which, she mused, subverted the guilt she had held at arm's length. *And anyway*, she thought, *you're not here to confess, you're here to pay tribute.*

Dolores (whose impeccable posture was the result of walking with a dictionary balanced on her head) thought about her family, which had assembled itself from disparate parts: Jewish immigrants from Austria, Catholics from Poland; its members had kept various secrets: common-law wives and illegitimate offspring, deaf children, illegal enterprises and honest ones. This small tribe's simultaneous vastness and insignificance was divided, vanished, impossible to contain. And now here she was in a church a stone's throw from Times Square, one of the loudest centers of iniquity, standing in front of a likeness of Mary, kindling a small fire to honor a mother she had abandoned and then lost, in that exact order. She needed to bury this fact as much as she needed to acknowledge it. These two urges, one engendering deceit, the other listing every reason such manipulation was unnecessary and too complex to sustain, competed every waking hour for Dolores's attention, which, she realized looking up at the face gazing down upon her, a face at once stern and impassive, needed to be turned to the task at hand.

How long, she asked herself, had it been since she had really prayed, not merely repeated the words taught in catechism, but since she had felt fervor when making her appeals? How long had it been since she truly believed there was a God who was listening? She tried to fasten her mind's eye to an accurate image of herself experiencing such devotional ardor, not to some cliché involving a slant of light beatifying the otherwise modest or childlike face of a saint. She was surprised to see Dolores the girl, age six, intently watching her maternal grandmother, Margaret, hem a woolen dress. In this image, snow fell in those perfectly crystalline flakes that fall in childhood memories, snow which was, her grandmother had taught her, the winter garment of God. Such an ordinary act, such graceful hands, such an absence of noise. And, she, Dolores, had paid attention.

What is prayer, she asked herself now, grasping simultaneously, if vaguely, that she didn't really know, might never know. What, asked the quickly shrinking honest part of her, what does a woman who no longer tells the truth pray for? And how would God respond to the supplications offered by a person for whom truth was so easily erased? Everything was so tangled.

"Blessed Virgin, please give solace to my mother," Dolores said. "And please tell David he should marry me," she whispered, unable to suppress this last request.

She gave the statue a final once-over, as if this wooden Mary were a real woman who had come to Slenderella to interview. Had she been able to travel through time and back, to stand there as the Dolores she was destined to become— bitter, depressed, lonely—she might have asked the mother of Christ the kinds of questions with sharp edges, questions Dolores was unpracticed at asking: "Well, what would *you* pray for, Mary, a different husband or a second child?" or "What kinds of little white lies does a virgin who's lost her only son have to tell to make it through the day?" or "How about you and your mother—why doesn't anyone blame you for abandoning her?"

What Dolores knew as she stood in that church, in the back of her self, under the terrible confusion crowding her psyche, was an injury that was far, far away from what her mother or grandmother had envisioned for her as a child. And, as to this austere wooden Mary in midtown Manhattan, what could she possibly know about a girl whose mother had missed (ignored?) and whose deaf grandmother couldn't stop the thing that had happened? Dorothy was dead, and Margaret was likely traveling today, Dolores figured, to the Catholic cemetery in Rochester, wearing dress lace-up boots she had worn as a young woman in 1920, a bouquet of white lilies in her hands.

DAY 5:
Take the Matter of Being Born

The days go I remain.
> —*Guillaume Apollinaire The Mirabeau Bridge, trans.*
> *by W. S. Merwin.*

And all at once the heart is blown to bits.
> —*E. Serebrovskaya, Mines, trans.*
> *by Babette Deutsch [June 4, 1939]*

I. "I shall never get you put together entirely"

At this point, you might want to back up a little because you are curious about Dorothy, wondering why Dolores, her only child, a capable and intelligent young woman with the means to send money or travel, had abandoned her at the time of her dying. You might imagine how Dorothy was the one to have catalyzed such a sorrowful cleaving between mother and child: Was it denial about Buxie and the secrets he surely had forced their daughter to keep? Was it jealousy? Or was it her own bitterness at having failed Dolores?

You might be tempted to return to a scene that unfolded in 1912 on Andrews Street in Rochester, to zoom in on Dorothy's own childhood, and, in particular, that moment when her mother, Margaret, with millinery of her own handiwork upon her head, escorted to St. Joseph's orphanage her little girl, a hearing child of deaf parents whose father had died and who had just started to realize that he was never returning and that she was different from her mother, a woman whose ears did not work. Later, much later, Dorothy realized that Margaret probably never felt as inadequate as at that singular moment, that she was as lost as any mother, unable to communicate that the choice to leave her daughter in the care of others because she was too poor to raise her was not a decision she knew how to explain to a young child.

Follow Dorothy through the years; watch her shoot up tall and lissome, her dark hair cropped short by the calloused fingers of the sisters because of lice and the unavailability of slower hands, the sort that might kindly braid a child's long hair. You'll see the shape of lengthening, bold legs that the nuns tsked about silently, tried, the best they could, to cover with all manner of long skirts, and confessed, if not to the priest then to God himself, that they envied. Dorothy was tall at a young age, and her height allowed her to form alliances with other girls, all of them lost in the oversized gray smocks and always too cold during the interminable winters in Rochester, what with the lake effect—cold northeast winds fetched by the warmer waters of Lake Ontario—and its ever-falling snow. In that long-legged girl who quietly peeled potatoes, washed floors, learned needlework, recited verses from the Bible, you might see the shape of the woman she would become.

After stepping into that particular and private history, which played out on an ordinary street on a day like any other, you might then appreciate how, when Dorothy finally left St. Joseph's, she left behind the one and only photograph her mother had pressed into her small hands the day they arrived at the door to the orphanage. She had kept the picture under her pillow at night, and by day it was pinned—at first by a caring young nun named Sister Agatha, then by Dorothy—to a flimsy chemise she wore beneath the woolen smock. The photograph showed her family—Albert, Margaret, and her—with her parents' friends, at Sodus Point. A summer memory. Ira Todd had made the photograph, capturing the very first word Dorothy had signed for her father, whose enthusiasm—he was embracing all the possibility in this particular moment—is expressed with raised arms and the grin of a man who has won a regatta. Father and daughter are captivated with one another. Margaret wears her signature hat and coy smile. All of them had filled up on watermelon that day, and happiness had been theirs. The water of Lake Ontario stretched far, Dorothy recalled, though she could not remember that summer save for the one image. And after she had lost the photograph, she wondered if any of it had been real.

At age twelve, Dorothy left the orphanage, returned home to Margaret, and started working as a seamstress, secreting away a coin here and there, readying, over the course of the next seven years, to leave. To Newark, New Jersey, where she met Saul, whom everyone called Buxie. She married him and delivered, on a just-new summer day in 1929, a baby girl. During the Depression, the new family squeezed with their in-laws into one small house at 176 Morris Avenue. Buxie's mother, Rose, kept Kosher, and Dorothy observed and then practiced the intricacies of separating meat from dairy, maintaining two sets of dishes, eliminating certain foods. But Buxie's mother refused to eat from the dishes of a Gentile. Her husband, Jacob, a window cleaner who learned to appreciate beauty from having looked inside so many rooms, was fond of sampling his daughter-in-law's fine pierogi, which she made with ground lamb instead of pork, though she could not cotton on why the flesh of baby animals was Kosher and that of grown pigs was not.

"Don't try to know what's unknowable, Dottie," Jacob said, sitting at the small table in her kitchen. The baby was asleep. She poured two cups of coffee, untied her apron, and sat.

Her father-in-law ate the last dumpling on his plate and sighed. For a large man, he had unusually slender fingers. His hands, had he been the violinist his son had trained to be, would have been delicate and aristocratic. But years of water, soap, bucket handles, and rags had calloused and scarred them. And strengthened them too, though his daughter-in-law knew, watching him hold her baby, that they were tender and child loving.

Dorothy wanted just then to ask him if he knew who his son really was, but instead, she sipped her coffee and wondered if she was ever going to feel fulfilled. And slowly, she started to consider and gauge the choices her mother had faced and how, for a widowed, deaf woman during the first two decades of the twentieth century, caring for a child meant extra complexity: how money was sometimes hard to come by, no matter how much you needed it, or that infants were demanding, and that it was easier to solve their necessities if you lived with extended family, which was something Margaret never experienced once her beloved husband, Albert, had died. Dorothy began to ponder her parents' union and as she came to appreciate the rarity of its completion and the tragedy of its severance, she wished she could will herself to reach through the shadows of memory to snatch back the lost image of that afternoon at Sodus Point. She was beginning to know, too, the spectrum of conditionality imposed or alleviated by love. Buxie, she had discovered soon after the earliest part of their courtship, was not an honest man, which meant he could never be honestly intimate with anyone, though Dorothy was also going to learn that children can be accomplices.

Dolores was seven when her father enlisted her as his "little helper." Tall for her age, she was often mistaken as an older girl, and this at a time, 1936, when maturity mattered. Until this point, Dorothy had been her daughter's primary parent—feeding her, teaching her basic skills and household chores, and sewing her clothing. Later, she liked to recall her child—the soft brown hair and slender, long-legged shape, the girlishness untouched and the beauty fresh and unambiguous—just before that first excursion into Buxie's hustle. There she was, one of so many children, who came up "just the other side of poor," as her mother-in-law, Rose, liked to say, in a nation brought to its knees by drought and economic depression. Dolores, whose aliases emerged in this environment, quickly learned the utility of disguising one's age, and the the more closely she observed these small transgressions of truth, the more she proved to herself that they were rewarded, if not with the pleasure of being virtuous, then at least with material gain.

Peppermints. Store-bought dresses and satin ribbons to secure her braids. Ankle socks and Mary Jane shoes. Silver-handled brushes and tortoise-shell hair combs, the stuff of fairytales. Shiny pennies and nickels pressed into the palm. She couldn't have enough of any of it.

Dorothy watched the unchilding of her daughter progress rapidly, feeling powerless to prevent the thievery that resulted. In less time than it requires to walk from a house in Newark to an automobile waiting on the street, Dolores transformed from a seven-year-old girl of mixed parentage—her grandfather liked to remind his family that in Nazi Germany at this time, such distinctions were of great import—to a miniature, much prettier, version of her father. To his swagger she added her own small swaying, always discreet, though discernible if you knew when to look. And to his fleshiness, she was as a sapling.

Dorothy had to look away.

One might attempt to trace the history of departures small and large in all the respective leave-takings in the generations of women that begin with Dolores's maternal great-grandmother, Mary, who begot and abandoned Margaret, who begot and surrendered Dorothy, who begot and relinquished Dolores, who begot and lost Kim, who is where the story ends and begins and ends again, over and over again and all at once. One might start to absorb the burden of abandonment passed down by each generation to the next and perhaps suspect the sequence was interrupted, the lineage stopped in its tracks by evolution itself, which one might come to think of—resisting the irony inherent in such contemplation—as the most intelligently designed phenomenon.

The last of Dolores is her daughter, me, and I have wanted to lay bare her life and examine it, to feel its fullness and emptying, to make sense of how a woman became who she was or how she came to be defined by what she did. People are always asking me to explain how I, the last in the line of daughters, managed to survive without becoming, say, a serial killer or, less dangerously, a perpetrator of fiscal crimes, and in reply, all I can offer is this tidbit of wisdom from people who work with child victims of violence: resilience depends on books in the home and the presence of at least one caring adult.

Narratives are always saving us, though because of the thread of complicity running from one generation to the next in my family, it makes sense that I've contemplated all manner of illegal and illicit exchanges and have even engaged in some minor ones. Such undertakings have meant lost sleep, travel in nightmares, and emotional landscapes whose bleakness induces thudding heartbeats and cold sweat. *Panikos*, from the Greek god Pan, who terrorized by making noises in the dark wood. It's no surprise that the metaphorical forest at night is the place with which I am most familiar; I came up in that ecosystem, with a mother who never once stepped foot, at least not that anyone knows or is alive to corroborate, in real woods.

II. *"so aloofly precise and so fragilely proud."*

Dolores created the kinds of stories which some might call lies. Her father was a large man, the kind of large that leaves itself behind, and from him she learned to tell lies that folks call *stories*, which because of elements such as plot and character and agency and narrative arc, is what people are most apt to believe. Saul Buxbaum, who became Stuart Buxton, had a gift for telling this sort of tale.

"Let me tell you about the land I have for sale," he starts. "A farmer worked that land, a great guy." He shakes his head. "He's elderly now, and his sons have all moved." He pauses for effect (everything in the story depends on artifice, after all). "To the city." (Here he may point his chin east, across the river, as if The City were always just the other side of the Passaic.) "All this fellow wants is to move to Wyoming, to be with his sister and her family." Another pause. "So he's selling it as is." He leans in closely to say the last pitch: "At a price you can afford."

The land is not Buxie's to sell. The buyer does not beware; the property, located far beyond sight, will be sold at this and each subsequent retelling of the story. Buxie will make a lot of cash, which he'll need when it comes time to uproot and relocate.

And how about Dorothy? Did she too spin myths of one sort or another after Dolores was born? In some secret part of her psyche, did she envision herself as some kind of Bonnie to Buxie's Clyde?

A black-and-white photograph shows the couple standing in a field in the late 1920s. Dorothy wears a blouse with cap sleeves and a skinny tie; her skirt is belted at the waist. Buxie's shirtsleeves are unevenly rolled, shirttails hastily (and in some places, barely) tucked into his trousers. He looks as if he was just awakened from a nap, which he was perhaps taking in the vehicle visible in the background of the image. Dorothy smiles in such a way that we assume she has some intimacy with the photographer. She stands tall, her presence diverting attention from the wrinkles in her skirt, which suggest long hours spent sitting (maybe in that car). Buxie poses as a flaneur, weight cocked to one side, his hip against hers. His expression dares the viewer to say something. The subject of that something is the woman around whose waist he has wrapped his right arm. "Want to tell me why she can't be mine?" he seems to ask. Or maybe he's thinking more along the lines of "Yeah, she *is* with me, buster" mixed with a bit of "You're sur*prised?*"

The tree line behind the couple ascends to the left. To the right the field seems to continue: open, flat, mown. The naked eye cannot discern the numbers on the license plate or the make and model of the automobile parked in the distance. The only people who know the place depicted in this photo are dead, which makes it a memory with no context, excorporeal, ungrounded, so far removed that it may as well be space debris. Yet I want to make something of this image, one of the few I possess of my grandparents as a young man and woman, because it depicts a moment before trouble came to define their lives and, ultimately, separate them.

I want to believe that the photographer—a girlfriend of Dorothy's? An associate of Saul's?—had returned from picking fruit in the woods beyond, a straw hat filled with blackberries, just as the couple had roused themselves from the sleepy summer loving that resulted in Dolores. I want Dorothy's smile to signal the beginning of a family-romance legend.

"This was taken the day we made you," Dorothy might have said to an eight- or nine-year-old Dolores, an age when girls are still girls who listen to and want to hear their mothers' stories. Or perhaps Dorothy wanted to say this but didn't, causing her daughter to mull over the image until the figures in it became so familiar they are unknowable.

And what *did* Dolores feel when she looked at this image of her parents? She knew their story better than I— she was there when Saul was taken away and when he left. She knew more intimately the conditions of their divorce. She followed *him*, left behind the mother whose beauty she never stopped trying to escape.

One daughter, then another, endows a picture with a message about enduring—persisting *and* bearing—intimacy. It renders Saul more vulnerable, his posture not one of a young bull wanting to lock horns with another but rather a response to having been wrecked by this dark-haired lovely. He will get even with her for having so ruined his bachelor heart. But neither of them knows that yet. She is barely twenty, the most beautiful woman he has ever met, and he is twenty-two, the most exciting man she will ever know. And they are living in New Jersey in the late 1920s right before the crash, both of them first-generation children of immigrants born on American soil. Saul's English is unaccented, and Dorothy's is spoken and not signed. They make a nice couple.

Regardless of whether Dolores was made before or after this image, the child will be named after sorrow, though why her mother has chosen this name will be unclear. The baby will spend her first years in the home of her grandparents, both of whom will dote on her, Jacob indulging her later with nickels and pieces of candy he keeps in his deep pockets, and Rose scavenging the tossed-aside clothing of the wealthy children whose parents employ her to clean and cook.

Buxie will call her Dizzy, insist that she's off in some way, maybe as a ruse to deflect his culpability. For what, one asks? Though I am the storyteller, I am, myself, unsure.

III. "the same bad dream goes on."

"My father never touched me," Dolores confides to me when Buxie dies. We are sitting, my mother on a small sofa, me in a faux-leopard, high-back chair in the living room of the apartment on West Seventieth Street. Ever the setting for things that become undone. We are listening to an album by Dory Previn. The television is on, its sound muted.

"What I mean…" my mother says, "is that he never held me."

For an instant, I sense that just the opposite is true. Maybe we weren't listening to Dory Previn; maybe I recall it that way because Dolores had explained, years prior, that Previn's "With My Daddy in the Attic" is about incest. I do not ask my mother to elaborate; I do not want to confirm this suspicion just now, though I am fairly certain I will one day wish otherwise. Either way, I think—if he touched her wrong or never held her—it's left a deep mark.

"Is there going to be a funeral?" I ask.

"I'm not going to it," she says.

We sit in silence. I look at the screen of the silenced television. In a commercial for Grecian Formula 44, the actor's hair looks as if it's coated with wax. I'm relieved that the sound is off.

"On my birthday in 1939, my father was arrested," Dolores tells me.

Words from this story will surface of their own accord, up from the brine of memory: *hiding, fear, suitcase.* Thirty-some years later, I will fashion from these disparate nouns a sequence of events, and though the connective tissue of the narrative is unstable, I will picture Dolores the morning of her tenth birthday, sitting at the kitchen table at 68 Norwood Street in Newark, New Jersey, outfitted in a store-bought white and blue taffeta dress with a chevron-shaped waist, a high, round neckline with buttons, and short puff sleeves. Her brown braids are tied with bits of satin ribbon. In a milk bottle on the table are a clutch of cornflowers.

Perhaps pancakes are being turned, Dorothy's hand gripping the wooden handle of the spatula, or maybe eggs are scrambling in a cast-iron pan. Dolores watches her mother move to the sink and imagines herself gliding from the stove to the faucet and mastering the utilitarian and mature female grace of the late 1930s, which she senses, even at ten, will become known as a lost time. Dorothy lifts her head to look out the open window. The-tire-on-gravel sound of an approaching vehicle grows louder, and the muscles in the back of Dorothy's neck tighten.

"Dolores," she says, turning toward her daughter. "Listen carefully to me." Dorothy's eyes are somber and deliberate. The smell of sunshine and bacon grease rises from the fabric of her apron. "And don't question what I tell you to do."

The girl feels a shadow passing over her face.

"Go upstairs and hide in your closet until I call for you," Dorothy says. She turns off the burners on the stove and removes the plates and utensils from the table. "Now."

Dolores slides her chair away from the table, rises, and leaves the kitchen. Each step of the narrow, rickety staircase seems to require an hour to conquer, though when she reaches the landing, the adrenaline that's turned up the volume of her pulse also seems to accelerate time. Her father is down the hall in the bathroom, shaving. The door is ajar. Though he is humming, she thinks she can make out the sandpapery sound of razor against whisker. Instead of going directly to her room and then the closet, she peeks into the bathroom at Buxie in undershirt, slacks, and shoes.

"Dizzy, I know you're there," he says. She sees his smile reflected in the mirror and pushes open the door.

"I love you, Daddy," she says. He pats her head with his free hand and then cups her chin in its palm, his fingers grazing her cheek almost imperceptibly.

"I know that," he says, the depth in his tone secure, reserved for the intimate. And before she knows it, he's removed his hand. The register of his voice fathers down a notch.

"What are you doing up here, anyway?"

She shrugs.

"Have you had breakfast?" he asks.

"I'm full already," she says, but later, she won't recall having told this little white lie.

He turns away from her and as he resumes shaving, Dolores goes down the hall to her bedroom, opens the closet, shuts the door, and sits in the corner, behind her mother's long wool coat, under the ruffles and hems of her own dresses. She inhales the odor of cedar and pretends she is as quiet as she imagines trees to be when no wind moves their branches. She doesn't really know the woods and doesn't plan to learn what it's like to walk in them. For

Dolores and her family, the forest is the province of the wild; they are working, urban folk, adapted completely from their villager and peasant forebears.

"Besides," Buxie likes to remind them, "a civilized person doesn't tromp around where there's no sidewalk."

She closes her eyes. "Say it, ever and ever so sweet, ever and ever so sweet just like an old valentine," she hears, though she knows no radio is broadcasting Frank Sinatra's crooning, and that she is the one making the sound happen in her head.

An insistent knocking on the front door echoes through the floorboards. Though the sounds are muffled, from the closet, Dolores can make out footsteps, male voices. Once they subside, her own heartbeat rises, and then a silence heavy with resignation, and finally, a dank smell, which startles her, of urine on cotton. She doesn't feel the wet until she shifts in the corner of the closet.

By the time Dorothy opens the door and stands like a monolith against the light, Dolores has removed her soiled undergarment, swabbed the floor, and hidden the sodden cloth in the corner opposite of where she crouched, intent on retrieving it once her mother is no longer in the room.

"I'm going to pack a suitcase, and we're going to see Nana in Rochester," Dorothy says, effectively altering Dolores's plan. As it turns out, she and her mother will never come back to this house in Newark.

No additional words are spoken. No explanations are offered. No meaning is made of the story for the girl named Dolores, a child of the Depression who believes just then, regardless of the peculiarities of her genealogy or the ruin of her underpants and pride, in fairytales and Hollywood endings. She promises herself she will find Buxie and bring him back, and the three of them will live happily ever after. Her magical thinking will not waiver, even after Buxie's sour breath first grazes her cheek.

On June 4, 1939, Dolores does not yet know how the characters in the story will collide with characters from other stories. Her father's father has not yet used his savings to buy fake passports and steamer tickets to liberate his cousins in Austria. Her father's mother has not yet discovered that her husband has an illegitimate son, whom Dolores will know as her first cousin. She cannot imagine Buxie in jail in Cincinnati through the next year, nor can she picture him coming to Rochester and living there for less than a year in 1941 before he divorces Dorothy and makes his way first to New York City and then west to California. Dolores is unable to foresee anything that happens next, though her daughter will later hazard to guess that in many ways Dolores not only clearly envisioned a particular future, she set herself deliberately on a path toward it.

Dolores experiences her father's arrest and his subsequent departures and second marriage as a long betrayal that she cannot absorb. There will be days—and though she cannot count them now, there will be at least five of them—during which she will arrange her own leave-takings. The first of which will be to flee, as soon as she is eighteen, the silence and damp cold of her grandmother's home in Rochester.

No one tells me how or when Buxie renames himself, or why and when Dolores follows suit. What I know is this:

In September of 1947, Buxie is arrested for loitering at a crooked dice game in Manhattan's Hotel Marguery on Park Avenue. He makes bail with money Dolores borrows from her boyfriend, Donnie, a young man who will go to war, return to Rochester to find his sweetheart departed, and never see repaid a dime of what he lent her.

After this New York City dice-game fiasco, maybe Saul Buxbaum and his daughter grift for a time between each of the country's coasts, slipping in and out of Mexico, whose sun and wildness stuns Dolores and keeps her focused on fabricating an urban self and life. Buxie dispenses with the name Saul and becomes Stuart, after an accountant he knew when he worked as a bona fide salesman in a Newark shoe store for a brief time. By the time Dolores is nineteen, she's dyed her hair platinum blonde. She seems, Buxie thinks, so settled in her new look, no longer the pretty girl next door from an upstate New York town, but the ingénue with a brash head of short curls and a hunger for attention. They both know that she will stretch the truth and say she's twenty-one. He figures that in another ten years, maybe even less, she'll be telling everyone she's a year younger.

As Buxie watches his daughter transform, he experiences his own metamorphosis. A first-generation Jew and only son, Stuart né Saul Buxbaum yearns to be, like so many of the Others of his generation, an American. *No blue blood in these veins*, he thinks, and as soon as he does, he knows that he and Dolores will become Buxtons, Stuart J. and Debbie, whose ancestors, they'll say if questioned, are buried in Great Britain, and who will lure their marks by assuming all manner of pretense they imagine to have inherited from their English forebears. He's so smooth, his daughter so electric, that his coolness and her heat will pretty much guarantee no inquiries will be made, no eyebrows raised.

"We'll be hidden in plain sight," Buxie tells his protégé, whom behind closed doors he still calls Dizzy. She, in turn, always thinks of him as her old valentine.

Though she'll forget that you're not supposed to fall in love with a mark, Dolores will remember the various deceits—distracting gamblers in pool halls and gentlemen in elevators so Buxie could relieve them of their wallets, and seducing married men who pay good money to keep an outraged father silent when he discovers them necking with his underage daughter at the back table of a hotel bar. She will watch how Stuart J. Buxton sells things he does not and never could own, parcels of land in New Mexico and bungalows in Florida; antiques shipping from Rome or Athens and art from Paris; and first editions procured in London and New York, "signed" by authors such as Mark Twain and Charles Dickens.

When Buxie tires of his daughter's company—his attentions will lock onto a blonde bombshell named Betty Lou, who comes complete with two blonde-bombshell daughters—he sets up Dolores with a fellow who's coming up in their world, a young man needing to rename and refashion himself. *A sharpshooter*, Buxie thinks, knowing that this David Neil—well, *his* name was different before, too—is exactly the guy to distract a dizzy young gal.

Debbie Buxton reinvents herself, re-emerging as Dolores Buxton, who leaves her father's side to apprentice in Hollywood salons and study the craft of concealment and the composition of expressions on a face. David Neil will propose to her, and they will make plans to move east. Dolores will go first, David will come later. *How facile it is to pretend to be someone else,* she thinks. A wig, some makeup, a costume, a little modulation of the voice, and voilà, you've created a persona. When at first she disguises herself, the artifice makes Dolores edgy. But once she sees how easy it is to create and inhabit a character, the adrenaline rush, that thing that propelled her up the stairs the day she turned ten, will have sunk its teeth into her and become, simultaneously, her first addiction and love. In one way or another, she has been rehearsing this role ever since she was born. She likes to think she will one day write the past out of her life. But in the short term, she has procured instead a ticket to New York City, a monogrammed alligator luggage set crammed with her clothing and makeup, some cash, a job, the promise of a ring on her finger, and a Manhattan apartment waiting for her to furnish it.

Right about here is where I discern the shape of a life lived between five distinct points. A pentagram of a lopsided star of a life. The entire motion of this life rising, as Rilke predicts, "from the depths of time," and falling back into the cavern of misplaced chronology and unkempt memory. Five days: the time it takes to complete a work or school week, about 1 percent of a year, 120 hours.

The characters in the story have been laid as bare as I can manage. Some things are best left unwritten, I think, though I am not sure I believe this.

AFTERWORD:
Through a Glass Darkly

" [...] The empty boudoir
Will haunt, but not how you imagine it will."

— *Sina Queyras, Sylvia Plath's Elegy for Sylvia Plath"*

In the weeks following my mother's death, insomnia ensued. On certain nights, determined to rest, I turned off the lights and raised the window shade. From my futon on the floor, with the covers pulled up to my neck, I looked up to the window. That rectangle was my companion until the sun paled its way into the sky, which made for a restless dozing, punctuated by burrowing under the bedding in search of a darkness gone absent. The window frame, its glass, and the fact of New York City scumbled yet churning beyond the pane (such a thin and transparent boundary) comforted me, but at the same time I was unable to stop staring at it, which of course kept me from sleeping. The play of headlights and streetlights cast moving shadows into my room and something about those distortions—their vague suggestion of solid matter that has become ethereal, perhaps—provided a temporary respite from despair. Life—and its constant exchange of love for sorrow, sadness for joy, poverty for wealth, fear for courage, and so on—took place beyond that window and, if one might call my insignificant huddle on the bed *living*, life was something one might see from the outside if one were to look into my room.

I tried to picture what might be seen from the rooms of apartments across the avenue: other buildings, of course; above, some truncated version of the sky; below, the cars and taxis and pedestrians and shop fronts, made miniature the higher one lived; there a rooftop and a shingled water tower against the day or night, dusk or dawn; behind, the pigeon communities in the airshafts between buildings; beyond, a river or a bridge. And who were they—what kinds of men and women, boys and girls, flora and fauna lived in all those places? Who among them was, like me, lying on the floor and contemplating a window whose shade was open, letting in the city-illuminated darkness?

Among the many lives I imagined while gazing at the glass rectangle night after night, the one life that should have been clear to me was my own mother's, yet her death was the event that trumped any contemplation of how she had truly lived. To parse out the motives for her final decisions was an exercise I refused during those very long hours when I yearned for less trouble, more love, a different perspective, an hour's sleep. The window both terrified me and provided solace—it requested of me neither decisions nor opinions and gave me no advice or judgment—so that I came to both loathe and desire it, though some part of me knew that such obsession with an architectural element indicated how ungrounded I was, how disconnected from the grieving I needed to engage but was unable to fathom.

Now, more than a quarter of a century later, to imagine Dolores's last hour, if only to honor her resolve, compels me. To purposefully stop your heart, you must be focused on completing what you begin, and following through was not in my mother's repertoire of how to live a life. And how can she be blamed for not knowing how to finish? She had known only uprooting—from girlhood, from places, from men, from her child—and the sum of all of it had undone her.

"I've written out things you should know. I hope you'll follow up," she wrote with no trace of irony, in her last earthbound note. I didn't follow up, nor did I do anything with her project ideas, which, along with the cosmetics line and the autobiographical miniseries called *Born Dead*, included an animated film based on a short story about a runaway sneaker I had written in sixth grade. If the last of Dolores's recorded ideas seemed like a bucket list of unaccomplished projects, to me they seemed like a to-do list I wouldn't want to manage. In a strange string of sentences—strange because of their inclusion in this, her suicide letter—she offered her ideas to stop drug trafficking, which involved legislated action to change tax codes and currency. By the time I reached the long disquisition about how the world was ready for a revival of *Arsenic and Old Lace* or the periodical glossy magazine called *Divorce* that Dolores had conceptualized, I could barely focus.

Contrast this lack of follow-through with the unerring premeditation of the suicide: My mother had organized in advance many details, such as changing her will two weeks before she died and adding Betty as executor and co-owner of the apartment, all this accomplished in her living room, made legal by the shady attorney who had, after she died, admonished me for being selfish. Dolores had easily procured the digoxin, for which she had a prescription, filled by Frank the pharmacist at the drugstore several doors down; John the porter likely fetched it for her (how could he have divined the purpose of this errand?). My mother had given away BG the Yorkie in early January. She had ordered new windows. At the end of February, over a month before she swallowed the pills that stopped her heart, Dolores had already written the twenty pages of instructions to me—which includes the list of six projects described in the eleven-page addendum to her original list of things she wanted me to "consider."

Here, then, is my mother readying her final, solo performance, which takes place on March 29, 1989, about noon, interior of apartment 4A. In her pink slippers, Dolores Eleanor Buxton pads down the brown-carpeted hallway to the kitchen, where she fills a glass with water from the sink's faucet, pads back to her bedroom, and places the glass on a coaster by her bedside.

She is neither thirsty nor hungry, and she has decided to forego her noonday breakfast of one half a frozen Lender's bagel and a cup of decaf coffee. All the ritualistic behavior ends today. There will be no more meals, each one planned to deliver just enough sustenance with the smallest caloric intake. There will be no more faces to put on, no more eyeliner, blush, or lipstick. No more disguising the scarred body with color-coordinated outfits. No more accessorizing. Even the pink slippers and the pilled bathrobe can be discarded. There will be no more walking down the hallway and back, no more bathroom trips in the middle of the night, no more daytime, afternoon, evening, late-night television. *The suicide will not be televised,* Dolores thinks, though she knows it's only a matter of time before her daughter will broadcast her own version of this episode. There will be no more envelopes with checks for John or Leonardo, no more letters or bills to stamp and mail or wait for, no more phone calls to make or not receive. No more messages on the answering machine to play or erase. Nothing to be dropped off or picked up. No more grocery lists or lottery numbers. *All the errands,* she thinks, *have been run.*

In spite of the framed photos occupying all the table surfaces in her bedroom—of her daughter, mostly, but also of her mother, her best friend, dead six months now, and her best friend's daughter—Dolores is alone. She is not going to die with a loved one's hand holding hers. She will not risk the retribution she believes she deserves: growing old, falling ill, and being ignored by her child, which is the thing she did to her mother, a burden she will lay down today.

"Forgive me, Mother," she might plead. Or instead, perhaps, Dolores will come to this place as a silent penitent, reveling in a quiet—not of apartment or city, but of mind— the likes of which she has never known.

She unties the bathrobe, hangs it over the chair in front of the vanity, and sits on the edge of the bed. Dolores will wear one piece of jewelry, a gold chain with a small gold charm, to her next destination, *wherever that may be,* she thinks, a bit coyly, but we must imagine something...well, if not good, at least playful here, lest the narrative become too cozily dark and melancholic. She reaches for the vial of digoxin next to the water glass and stops short when she realizes that another note is required; her daughter will not know to look for the small manila envelope she has deposited between the night table and the bed, a place that might go uninspected by someone as trustworthy as John or Leonardo, because they will not assume they must bend down to look for anything. They are men who stand straight and look in front of them, not down at the ground. And since she is sure that one of them will find her, she has taken care to mediate their sense of not having signed up for discovering a naked suicide by giving them each a very handsome Easter gift. No one in the building has ever given cash to the super or the porter at Easter, which Dolores dismisses as another one of her original ideas that no one will find particularly useful. There will be no more original ideas coming forth from her mind after today.

She rises, slips her feet into the terrycloth mules, and re-robes. Once again to the kitchen, where she retrieves and opens the spiral-bound notebook whose pages she has already used for the longer missive, which sits in its sealed envelope, propped up against the base of the night table in her bedroom. She sits at the desk in the kitchen and writes six sentences to her daughter, who will count the fifty-three words over and over again, a reckoning Dolores cannot visualize. She tears the page out of the notebook, which she returns to its spot on the shelf above the desk, and trundles back down the hallway, note in hand.

Once in her bedroom, she folds the note in half, twice, and leaves it on the bedside table. Dolores opens the drapes, astonished by the brightness of the light coming through the north-facing windows. She disrobes, hangs the natted pink polyester of her shut-in self over the chair, revels just the slightest in her nudity and how much more naked she feels in the presence of daylight, and sits on the edge of the bed. She is determined to complete this particular project, and with one quick maneuver of her arthritic fingers, she opens the bottle of digoxin and shakes out its contents into her hand. Dolores swallows the pills two at a time. After ten or twelve sips of water, she isn't counting anymore. She places the glass on the night table, aware she hasn't drained the liquid in it, but for once not caring that such an inconsequential thing is left undone. She figures that now, there is no turning back. *Well,* she thinks, *you could pick up the telephone and dial emergency,* but she knows she won't. Instead, Dolores stretches out on the bed and neglects to cover her breasts, which various men have admired, which she regretted not using to suckle her child, breasts whose silicone implants will be palpated in twelve hours by the coroner, another consequence she does not anticipate. She takes one last look at the ceiling, a surface whose every crack, however fine, and whose every blemish small and large she has memorized, as if this is her night sky and the constellation of smudge, plaster drip, and missed spot are the stars.

She looks then toward the dresser, fixes her gaze upon the unopened Chanel No. 5, which towers over the other perfumes. It had been a gift. From whom? She can no longer recall. Even without glasses, she can make out a thin line of dust on the bottle's cap and shoulders. This will not do. She sits up, plucks a tissue from the bedside box of Kleenex, crosses the room, and dusts the bottle. She returns to bed, disposing of the tissue along the way.

Dolores knows that in an hour or two, her heart will seize. She wonders if she will feel the cells die one by one, or if she'll be catapulted into nothingness. Will that oblivion be so dark she cannot see her hands in front of her, or will the light be so white it burns the eyes? Will she be able to hear or see what goes on after her spirit rises from her body, if it even does that? Dolores offers up her need to know what might next take place. She thinks instead of what she believes will happen after her heart and breathing stop. About an hour after she dies, she is certain that it won't be Leonardo, but John, making his 3:30 call, who will ring the bell and knock at the same time, as he always does, unlocking the door and letting himself in after waiting exactly four and a half minutes for her to answer.

"Miss Buxton," he'll call out. Dolores will miss the sweet air of his voice.

When he doesn't hear her respond, what will he do? she wonders. Will he call out again? Will he wait and call again?

Will he hold his hat in his hands as he makes his way down the hallway? *He doesn't wear a hat, silly.* Dolores smiles, though she doesn't know that her mouth will not be smiling when she is discovered. She pictures John as if he were a movie star—Henry Fonda or Jimmy Stewart or Clark Gable before the confident male swagger of first maturity, a thing she has missed for so long that it surprises her to behold it at this particular moment. She imagines him in a sentimental picture whose lead male character is young and green and holds his hat in his hand while making his way down the hallway of an apartment belonging to a sophisticated New York woman who has been courted by celebrities and powerful people and played backgammon with wealthy sheiks, produced films, and dined with presidents. A woman who was born across the river, lived north, went west, came east, settled here on this crowded island. And all this only to entertain the audience of a building's porter come to deliver the mail.

ACKNOWLEDGMENTS

For encouraging me to write this story and for reading it in its many iterations, I am grateful to Dustin Beall Smith. For believing in the book once it was written, my deepest gratitude goes to Robert Wilson, Peter Nichols, Howard Norman, Eugenia Kim, Sean Carp, Elizabeth Earley, Lily Hoang, and Jaded Ibis Press. For helping make this book come true, with their hands-on and/or spiritual assistance, I am thankful to the gifted and eagle-eyed Kate Gorton; the generous and talented Eugenia Kim; my dear friends Mary E. Lide, Robin Powell, Sarah Stromeyer, Roberta Gordon, and Rick Greenberg; and my dearest heart Penelope Anne Schwartz. I was blessed to have the company of three four-legged companions while composing this narrative, and though they are no longer alive, I am grateful to the love and sustenance provided me by Max, Bliss, and Queenie. I've certainly left out someone, and for this oversight, I apologize.

Most of Section II of Day 2 was originally published as "Habeas Corpus" in *Ninth Letter*, 4.1 (Spring 2007); the essay was reprinted in *I Just Lately Started Buying Wings: Missives from the Other Side of Silence* (Graywolf Press, 2010).

Titles of sections and subsections derive from the following sources:

9   Alex Dimitrov, "The Last Luxury, JFK, Jr."

21   Day 1 Title: John Donne, "This Is My Play's Last Scene"

23   Section I: Ludwig Wittgenstein, *Notebooks*

Cover photos courtesy of author. Top, Dolores, Rochester, ca. 1947; center, Dolores, ca. 1949; bottom, upside down, Dolores, ca. 1953.

This is a work of mostly nonfiction. Names and facts have been preserved and the chronology of events is unaltered. However, in an effort to get at the truth, I've had to imagine certain moments in the lives of the characters who figure in this narrative.

COVER ART BY
Eugenia Kim

The typeface family used in this book is
Weiss